HERBS

FOR BETTER LIVING

Recipes by Janice Baker

Text: Louise Egerton
Editor: Ingaret Ward
Gardening Consultant: Frances
Hutchison
Herb Consultant: Paul Callinan
Design Concept: Deborah Johnston
Art Director: Ivy Hansen
Assistance: Elizabeth McLeod

Photography: Ashley Barber,
Denise Greig and Lorna Rose
Food Styling: Janice Baker and
Michelle Gorry

Published by Bay Books
61–69 Anzac Parade,
KENSINGTON NSW 2033

© Bay Books

National Library of Austrâlia
Card Number and ISBN 1 86256 386 1

BB89

Printed in Singapore by Toppan Printing Co.
(S) Pte. Ltd.

The publisher would like to thank the following
for their assistance during the production of
this book: Common Scents Cottage Dural, for
herbs, flowers and roses; Corso de' Fiori Pty
Ltd for tableware; Keyhole Furniture for cane
furniture; Les Olivades, for tableware and
cushions; Weldon Trannies for transparencies.

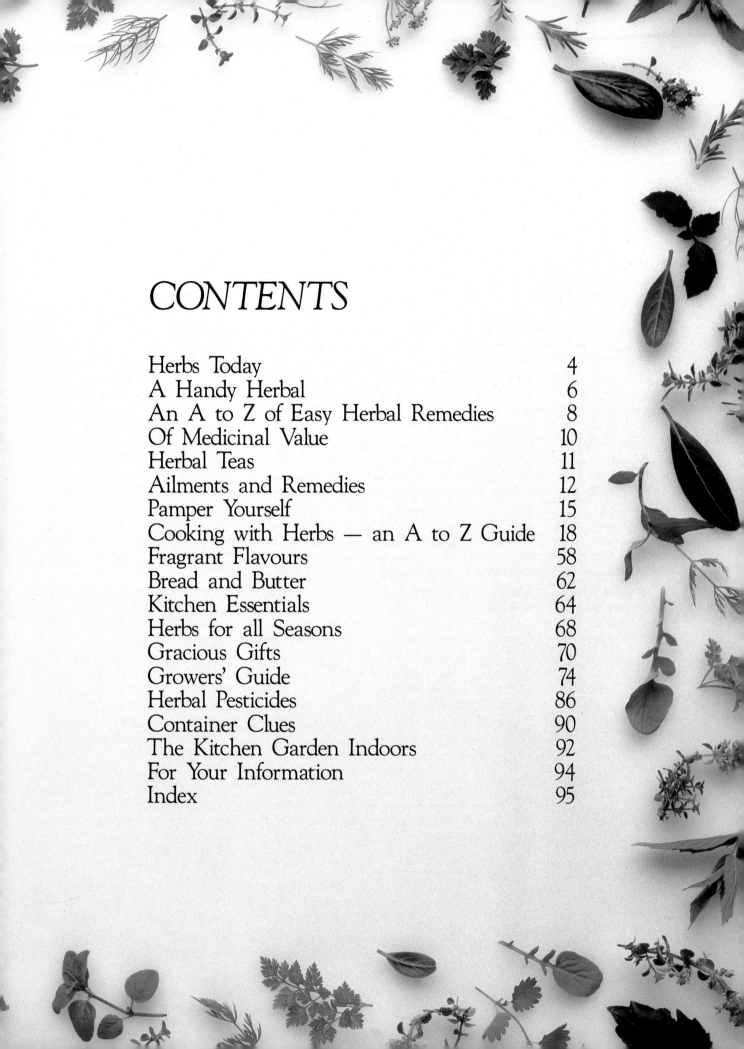

CONTENTS

HERBS TODAY

For generally delicate, easily bruised and often rather insignificant looking foliage, herbs pack a punch.

Over thousands of years, herbs have been transformed into soothing balms, delicious teas, perfumes, dyes, wines, natural pesticides, medicines and often vital recipe ingredients; their aromatic qualities and taste cannot be successfully synthesised or copied, by even the smartest twentieth-century chemists.

Herbs like mint, sage, thyme, bay tree, caraway and coriander were known in Egypt and the Middle East in Biblical times. Fenugreek, anise and saffron were prized for their usefulness in the kitchen. Some herbs even came in handy for the occasional bit of embalming.

The Ancient Romans were also great fans of herbs and, as they systematically conquered the known world, they brought their habits — and their herbs — with them.

As Christianity took a foothold in Europe, and the monasteries started to spring up, monks took over the cultivation of herbs, often combining them to make powerful remedies.

The popularity of herbs continued unabated until the middle of the nineteenth century. Fifteen hours down the mine or working heavy machinery from dawn to dusk removed any incentive, and available time, to work in the garden cultivating herbs.

Gardens themselves diminished. Inner city houses, built for workers, had tiny or non-existent gardens. They had useless courtyards, at best.

With industrial 'progress' over the next decades, came the perceived need for convenience foods, preservatives, pre-processed foods, additives, canning, synthetic 'flavour enhancers', freezing and freeze-drying of food. The whole notion of growing and harvesting what you needed, at the time you needed it, came to be seen as old-fashioned, almost anti-progress.

The pendulum not only swung, it bowled many people over in the 'sixties. The aptly named flower power of the hippies provoked people to re-assess what was actually happening around them. While considered dangerously radical, or at least the lunatic fringe, by many at the time, hippy views about natural food and health have virtually become collective wisdom in the late 'eighties.

We are now increasingly aware of what we have done to the ozone layer and the food chain. Soil erosion, polluted air and water — nobody would call concern about these facts 'radical thinking' any more.

Thus have herbs come full circle. In the 'fifties, only the most adventurous cook would have craved anything more than mint 'and a little parsley for decoration' outside the kitchen door. Views and tastes have changed so radically, and Asian food in particular has taken such a hold on our tastebuds, that lemon grass, thyme and coriander would be mere staples in many herb gardens today.

An added bonus is that most herbs can be grown in tubs (a boon for tenants and others who are regularly on the move) and in the smallest of spaces, as long as sun is plentiful. A sunny windowsill can yield a decent bouquet garni in a matter of weeks.

Retail nurseries and mail order houses now despatch herb seeds and plants all over the nation. And as for dried herbs! Even the humblest corner store has a stock of bottled herbs and spices that would startle our grandmothers.

The natural qualities of herbs are once again prized. The search for taste and nutritional value, a growing abhorrence of the synthetic and the chemical, and a healthy distrust of the medical profession's love affair with drugs, have made cultivation and use of herbs one of the most popular gardening, health and cooking trends today.

We trust this book will help you to discover some of the joys of growing and using your own herbs. We know you'll be amply rewarded when you lift the lid off what used to be your standard chicken casserole, enticing herbal aromas drift through the air, and you get knocked over in the rush to the table!

Above: Herbs like sage, chives, thyme, marjoram and parsley grow well in tubs

Left: Herbs such as spearmint, eau-de-cologne mint, lavender and pink sage, look decorative and grow well in the garden

HERBS AND SPICES — WHAT'S THE DIFFERENCE?

Botanically, herbs are soft-stemmed, annual, biennial or perennial plants which die back after flowering. In common usage, the term 'herbs' refers to plants containing aromatic substances and which are used for flavouring, for perfumes or for medicinal purposes.

In cooking, a distinction is made between spices and herbs. Spices are derived from the root, bark or fruits of perennial plants such as pepper, nutmeg and cinnamon and are commonly used in a dry powdered form. On the other hand, herbs are derived from the leaves (and sometimes the flowers) of usually shrubby, annual, biennial or perennial plants. The seeds of a few herbs — anise, caraway, coriander and dill — are also used in cooking.

Left: Basil and garlic are superb kitchen herbs

Above: Add fresh mint to your summer fruit salads

5

A HANDY HERBAL

For thousands of years, herbs have been used to cure various ailments. From Ancient Egypt and the Classical world of Rome and Greece, to Persia, India, China and Russia, herbs formed the basis of all medicine. In the Western world, medieval monasteries and hostels always had herbal gardens, from which they made ointments and infusions to treat local people.

Many manuscripts exist on herbal medicines. In 1550, the Chinese scientist Li Shi Zhen, published 52 volumes on the use of herbs and spices in Chinese medicine.

Other tomes of wisdom include Culpeper's *Herbal* (1616–1634), a collection of herbal remedies, and *The Truth about Herbs*, written by Mrs Leyel, whose enthusiasm sparked the formation of a Society of Herbalists in London in 1936.

In many countries, a form of herbal-based medicine still exists, and the Western world is experiencing a revival of interest in their use.

Many of the effects of herbal medicines are gentle and cumulative. Those taken as a general health tonic can be particularly slow but taken regularly, as part of your diet, their efficacy will gradually be felt.

In the case of complex herbal preparations it is very often easier, less time consuming and cheaper to buy them from a chemist or health food shop, than to make up something yourself.

WONDER WEEDS

As we all know, prevention is better than cure. Keep your body healthy and you need never concern yourself with cures. So let's look at some effective ways to use herbs that will keep you fighting fit.

DANDELIONS
TARAXACUM OFFICINALE

Of the several herbs with an impressive number of useful properties, dandelion comes top of the list, with just about everything your body needs. For black coffee and alcohol drinkers, dandelion should be used as a preventative measure. Dandelion's vitamin A content helps replace lost vitamin A to the liver. You need vitamin A to help combat infection, which is why drinking is said to lower your resistance.

Eat the leaves raw in salads or drink dandelion coffee, made from the root and available from most health food stores. A cup of dandelion coffee each day is an excellent way of keeping your liver in good working order.

Besides vitamin A, dandelion also contains vitamins B1, B2, C and choline, another regulator of the liver. The leaves contain iron, copper, silicon, magnesium, sodium, and substantial amounts of calcium; also potassium and phosphorus which maintain a healthy nervous system, and sulphur, an excellent body cleanser. With all this, dandelion is a real 'wonder weed' and the best news is, it's freely available in waste ground, pavements and gardens, so make the best of it. One tip: don't pick dandelion leaves around telegraph poles — the wood preserver is toxic and sometimes seeps into the surrounding ground; also it's a favourite spot for doggies.

There is a plant that grows side by side with the true dandelion and looks remarkably like it but it is a fake. The true dandelion has pale green, soft leaves with no hairs. The leaves are deeply indented and the flower is borne on a single stem from the centre of a rosette of leaves. The masquerading dandelion also forms a rosette of leaves but they are hardly indented at all and are hairy, shiny and a darker green. The flowers are borne on a dividing stem. This plant has no known benefits to the human being.

PARSLEY
PETROSELINUM SATIVUM

This favourite culinary herb can also help those with kidney or bladder problems. Parsley leaves and roots contain apiol, which acts as a diuretic, cleansing the kidneys of waste products. A few sprigs of raw parsley each day will keep you well in this department. Parsley is also well noted for its high levels of vitamins A, B1, B2 and C, and the mineral iron. It should be a regular item in every health-conscious diet.

NASTURTIUMS
Tropaeolum majus

These colourful plants have antibacterial qualities, too. Eat the flowers and leaves in salads to combat colds, flu or chest infections.

RED CLOVER
Trifolium pratense

A fairly common herb, its iron and copper content is useful for improving blood circulation. It is also recommended for coughs, colds and asthma. You can make a good tea from fresh or dried flowers or the top leaves: boil for 5 minutes to extract the iron and copper.

HORSERADISH
Armoracia lapathifolia

This is another general health-giver. It purifies the blood and clears the body of superfluous mucus. It is particularly useful for sinus sufferers, and taken on a regular basis, will help keep the sinuses clear. Available from the chemist in tablets or capsules, small quantities of finely grated fresh root can also be steeped in vinegar and water, no more than two teaspoons a day.

WATERCRESS
Nasturtium officinale

Another multi-purpose natural weed is watercress. Watercress is an excellent guardian against bacterial infections, so eat plenty of it, especially in winter when colds and flu abound. Eat the tasty leaves and stalks raw and washed — the slightly peppery flavour is delicious in salads.

GARLIC
Allium sativum

This is a natural antibiotic and antiseptic. Garlic is good for many things including colds and heart disease. High in sulphur, iron and calcium, it can clear the body of infection, so make it a regular part of your diet. You can either eat a raw clove of garlic a day or, to avoid smelling just like what you ate, take it in odourless capsule form, available from chemists and health food stores. It can be taken in quite large quantities when infection strikes — up to 20 capsules a day — but it is not recommended for people with bad liver, gall or bile conditions.

Fresh herbs are both decorative and useful

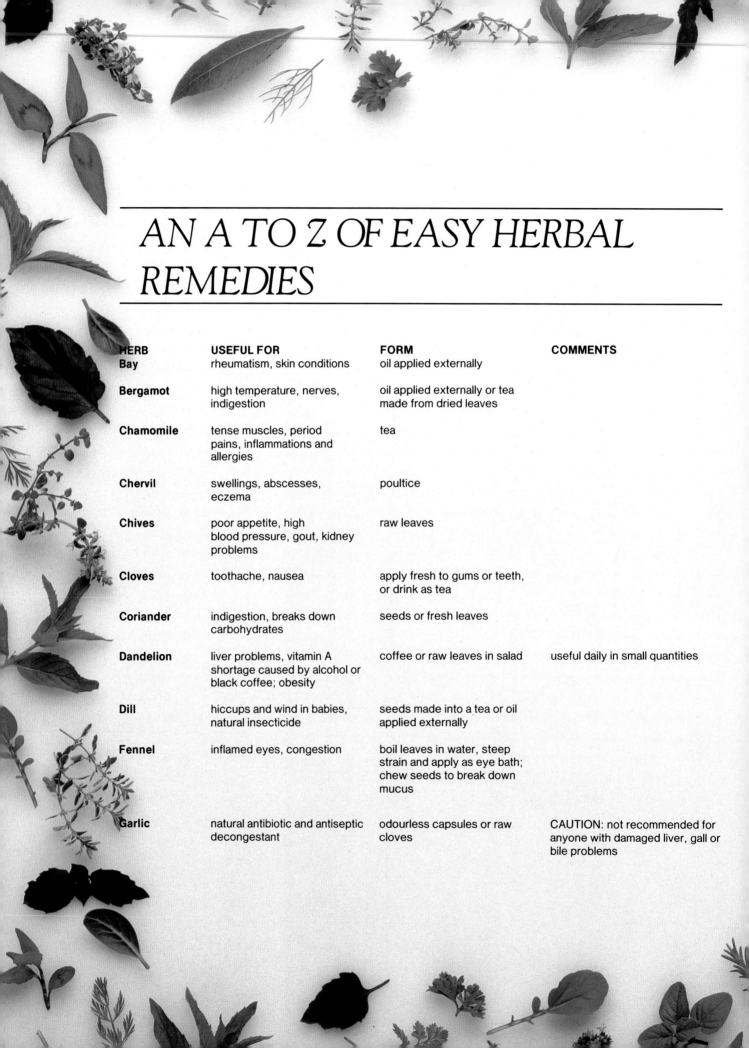

AN A TO Z OF EASY HERBAL REMEDIES

HERB	USEFUL FOR	FORM	COMMENTS
Bay	rheumatism, skin conditions	oil applied externally	
Bergamot	high temperature, nerves, indigestion	oil applied externally or tea made from dried leaves	
Chamomile	tense muscles, period pains, inflammations and allergies	tea	
Chervil	swellings, abscesses, eczema	poultice	
Chives	poor appetite, high blood pressure, gout, kidney problems	raw leaves	
Cloves	toothache, nausea	apply fresh to gums or teeth, or drink as tea	
Coriander	indigestion, breaks down carbohydrates	seeds or fresh leaves	
Dandelion	liver problems, vitamin A shortage caused by alcohol or black coffee; obesity	coffee or raw leaves in salad	useful daily in small quantities
Dill	hiccups and wind in babies, natural insecticide	seeds made into a tea or oil applied externally	
Fennel	inflamed eyes, congestion	boil leaves in water, steep strain and apply as eye bath; chew seeds to break down mucus	
Garlic	natural antibiotic and antiseptic decongestant	odourless capsules or raw cloves	CAUTION: not recommended for anyone with damaged liver, gall or bile problems

Ginger	colds and flu, cleanses system	tea made from ½ teaspoon powdered ginger in 1 cup boiling water. Add honey and brandy, if desired	
Horehound	colds and flu	use dried leaves in a tea with honey	
Horseradish	purifies blood; clears mucus and sinus; good all-round tonic	capsules or as a vinegar syrup or poultice	CAUTION: small quantities only; stop immediately if vomiting or diarrhoea occurs
Lavender	rheumatism, muscle pain, headaches, stings	oil applied externally	
Marjoram	rheumatism, muscle pain, toothache	oil applied externally, or fresh leaves, chewed	
Nasturtium	antibacterial properties, useful against colds and flu	fresh flowers or leaves used in salads	CAUTION: seeds not recommended because of high oxalic acid content
Parsley	diuretic that helps bladder, kidneys; bad breath	fresh leaves	a must in any health-conscious diet
Pennyroyal	natural insecticide, period pains, nausea, headache	grow near verandahs or dog kennels; tea made from dried leaves	CAUTION: all types of mint should only be taken in small quantities by pregnant women
Red clover	iron and copper content improve blood circulation; ease coughs and colds	tea made from topmost leaves, fresh or dried flowers	
Rosemary	tension headache, hair conditioner	oil rubbed into scalp or used as a hair rinse	CAUTION: large quantities of fresh or dried herb taken internally, can cause poisoning
Sage	toothache, bleeding gums, rheumatism, grey hair	tea or fresh leaves, rinse applied to hair	CAUTION: avoid large quantities if pregnant or breastfeeding
Sorrel	boils	poultice	CAUTION: large quantities taken internally can cause poisoning, so avoid teas
Thyme	headache, throat infections, indigestion, bowel disorders	oil applied externally, tea	CAUTION: large quantities taken internally can cause irritation
Yarrow	cuts and grazes	leaves pressed to injured area	CAUTION: can cause allergic skin reaction in some people

OF MEDICINAL VALUE

These practical preparations, all quite simple and requiring no special equipment, encourage herbs to release their medicinal properties. They make interesting, effective alternatives to chemicals, and are useful for minor ailments.

Dandelion tea

TINCTURES

A preparation of herbs in alcohol. Rubbing alcohol or vodka is normally used. The usual proportions are 40 g crushed or powdered herb to 600 mL alcohol. Put the two ingredients together in an airtight bottle or jar, filled to the top, leave in a warm place and shake the container every day for 3–4 weeks. The tincture is then ready for use. Tinctures have a long shelf-life and are therefore more useful than decoctions, which only last a short while.

OILS

Another way to encourage herbs to release their properties, by steeping them in oil. Take a jar of vegetable oil and fill it with crushed herbs. Leave it in a sunny or warm place and shake it each day for a couple of weeks. Strain off the herbs and repeat the process with some fresh herbs for another 4 or 5 weeks.

OINTMENTS

Herbs simmered with either lard or petroleum jelly. It is usually simpler to buy these preparations from a health food store.

INHALATIONS

A few drops of oil essence, dropped into a bowl of steaming hot water. The idea is to breathe in as much of the steam as possible through the mouth and nose. Bend over the bowl with a towel over your head to trap the steam.

POULTICES

A preparation of chopped or crushed herbs wrapped in cheesecloth and applied to a sore spot as hot as you can bear it. Place the herbs in the centre of the piece of cheesecloth, twist it up and tie with string, then dunk the herb bag into a pan of boiling water. Make sure you have the edges of the cheesecloth dry and poking out of the pan, so you can pull it out when the herbs are mushy. Squeeze out any excess moisture and apply immediately to the sore spot. Either hold it there until it cools or bandage it in position. This treatment draws the poisons out of an infected area, soothes inflammations, and promotes healing.

COMPRESSES

Like a cold poultice. Apply lint saturated with a cold herbal infusion, to the infected part and remove when it has become warm. Apply another cold, infusion-laden piece of lint and repeat until you feel relief. Compresses are usually used to reduce swellings, such as bruises and black eyes.

DECOCTIONS

The preparation of boiled bark or root of a herb. The bark or root should be washed and then the bark crushed and the roots grated or chopped. The herb is left to simmer, covered in a pan, until the fluid reduces. Sometimes it is left to cool and steep for 12 hours before the liquid is strained off to provide the decoction. This is often a long-winded operation and is not commonly practised in the home these days.

A WORD OF WARNING
The scientific basis of herbal medicines is still under investigation. Always heed cautionary notes attached to any product or plant description, and never take more than the recommended dosage. Too much of any herb can be dangerous. If you suffer from a medical condition, *always* check with your doctor or local chemist before taking anything.

It must be remembered that self-help herbal treatments should be used only for mild infections and illnesses. If you are seriously ill, consult your doctor or a professional alternative practitioner, if you prefer.

Finally, if you collect herbs from waste ground or beside motorways and you are not absolutely sure whether a herb is what you think it is, get it professionally identified by a botanist or herbalist before going ahead with any treatment. Many plants look like other plants, and it takes time to become proficient at recognising what is what.

HERBAL TEAS

These refreshing alternatives are low in tannin and mostly caffeine-free. Whether you choose chamomile tea to get a good night's sleep or fennel to aid your digestion, you can enjoy the refreshing taste of these natural remedies.

Herbal teas are not only curative and soothing, natural tranquillisers which can calm the nervous and digestive systems, they taste good too! If you have a mass of a particular herb growing all over the garden, you will probably have enough leaves or flowers to collect for a good-size packet, tin or box of tea.

They make excellent presents. Save any packaging that you think might make an attractive tea caddy but remember, to keep the tea's flavour, lids must be airtight. Label the tea container and decorate it if you wish. You may like to add some information about the herb tea and what it is used for.

INFUSIONS AND TEAS

Dried or fresh herbs left to steep in boiling water. Many herbal teas have a soothing, refreshing or stimulating effect on the body, and provide a gentle method of treatment which is easy and inexpensive. Most produce excellent flavours, though some are a little bitter. If this is the case, add a little honey to sweeten.

Herbal teas can be drunk hot or cold. Usually the leaves or flowers of the herb are used to make tea but occasionally seeds are used. To extract their goodness, crush seeds with a pestle and mortar before use.

Preparing a herbal tea is like making any other kind of tea. You can use dried or fresh herbs. If using dried herbs, the usual proportions are: 1 teaspoon to each cup of boiling water. If you are using fresh herbs, use three times the quantity of herb. Fresh herbs should be lightly crushed, chopped, or bruised before putting in the teapot, in order to extract their therapeutic properties. A china teapot is most suitable and aluminium should be avoided. Leave the infusion to steep for 5–6 minutes. Many herbal teas become bitter if left to steep too long.

Above: Sage (Salvia officinalis)

Left: A selection of herbal teas

11

AILMENTS AND REMEDIES

Herbal remedies used for centuries are currently coming back into favour. Herbalists and naturopaths often make up their own medicines, and can also be consulted if you wish to experiment and try making some remedies yourself. If in any doubt, always consult a qualified medical practitioner.

BORAGE AND COMFREY: A CAUTIONARY NOTE

Borage (*Borago officinalis*) and comfrey (*Symphytum officinalis*) are often recommended as herbal treatments for, respectively, reducing fever and nervous conditions; and relieving colds, bronchial and tubercular conditions.

However, both these herbs are currently under investigation by the Australian National Health and Medical Research Council. It is thought that the pyrrolizidine alkaloids they each contain, may cause liver damage and cancer. Pending results, they may be listed as poisons. Their use, therefore, is definitely *not recommended* until further information is available.

ABRASIONS OR SEPTIC WOUNDS
Warm Calendula (marigold flowers) in boiling water or tea tree oil and apply as a poultice.

AGEING SKIN
Rosemary oil, rubbed into wrinkles, is said to be effective. Apply just before going to bed.

APPETITE STIMULANT
Chives, they say, make you hungry.

BAD BREATH
Chew a few sprigs of parsley or drink rosemary tea.

BALDNESS
Nettle tea made from dried or fresh leaves applied to a balding scalp can, in some cases, lead to hair regrowth.

Above: Marigolds (Calendula officinalis)
Below: Sorrel (Rumex acetosa)

Above: Purple-flowered borage (Borago officinalis)

Lorna Rose

DID YOU KNOW?
- Rubbing some lavender oil into your muscles before a bushwalk or any vigorous exercise will prevent them from seizing up.
- To avoid being bitten to death by mosquitoes, rub your bare skin with pennyroyal leaves before venturing out.
- If your dog suffers from fleas, plant pennyroyal around its kennel: this will repel them.
- To keep your dog's kidneys in good working order, chop a few parsley leaves into its food about twice a week.
- To keep your dog worm-free, chop a little garlic and horseradish leaves into its food every few days.

BRONCHIAL INFECTIONS
Provided you do not suffer with liver, gall or pancreas problems, garlic will ease bronchial infections that are caused by bacteria. To help you breathe, use peppermint oil, either as an infusion or with a few drops in a handkerchief or tissue (keep peppermint oil away from noses and eyes as it can burn). The fumes are very powerful and will loosen phlegm, calm the bronchial nerves and induce sleep. Eucalyptus oil rubbed on the chest is also good, but keep away from eyes, nose, lips and ears as it, too, burns. For bronchitis and chest complaints, eat horehound leaves, mixed with honey, to clear congestion. Mullein or cow lungwort, which grows on waste ground, can ease lung infections and asthma. Make a tea from the flowers and leaves: (add 1 handful to a cup of boiling water, leave to stand for 1 hour, strain and drink. This also makes a good inhalation. Mustard baths can also help clear congestion.

BRUISES
Chervil leaves in a poultice will help reduce swelling. You can also apply hyssop leaves as a poultice: twist them into a piece of cheesecloth and steep in hot water for 5 minutes. Apply as hot as possible. This should reduce the swelling and reduce the dark colour.

CATARRH AND CHEST CONGESTION
This can be eased with hyssop leaf tea. Horseradish clears mucus. Anise, fennel and garlic are also good decongestants.

CHILBLAINS
Take 1 teaspoon cayenne pepper, stir into a little hot water and apply as a poultice.

BITES AND STINGS
Nettle ointment will reduce the pain of ant and bee stings, tick bites, mosquitoes and fly bites. It can alleviate many skin irritations, such as scratches or cuts. Crushed savory leaves will also lessen the pain of a bee sting.

BLACKHEADS AND PIMPLES
Fenugreek tea will encourage the sweating out of many impurities clogging the skin. It smells a bit like curry but don't be discouraged. The seeds of fenugreek are more efficacious than the powder.

BLOOD PRESSURE, HIGH
Members of the onion family can help break down cholesterol, so eat plenty of onions, garlic, chives, leeks and shallots.

BOILS
Make up a poultice of French sorrel leaves. This will help to bring up the boil and speed the process of extracting the poison.

Fennel (Foeniculum vulgare) *in flower*

COLDS AND FLU
As soon as you feel the first indication of an approaching cold, eat 10 or so white horehound leaves, taken with a little honey to counteract the bitterness. If you eat some more later it will not harm you, and some people believe it to be a reliable cure. Try it and see for yourself. If the infection is already upon you, you can accelerate the process by making yourself the following drink: a couple of crushed garlic cloves, fresh lemon juice, a little grated clear lemon rind, ½ teaspoon powdered ginger and a pinch of cayenne added to boiling water; drink as soon as it is cool enough and go straight to bed. Just sweat it out and wait. In combatting some strains of flu, the sulphurous content of watercress can be most medicinal as well.

CRACKING FINGERNAILS
Take horsetail (*Equisetum arvense*) tablets. Horsetail contains high quantities of silicon, as well as calcium, sodium and iron.

CUTS AND GRAZES
Scented geraniums crushed and applied as a poultice, make a good antiseptic. Also the antiseptic yarrow leaf, pressed to the cut, will staunch the flow of blood and hasten the formation of scar tissue: try this when you nick yourself shaving. Hyssop leaf poultice is another healer.

DIGESTIVE PAIN, UPSET STOMACH, GASTRIC INFLAMMATION, GASTRIC ULCER
Take a nutritious and soothing drink made from 1 teaspoon slippery elm powder added to a little cold water. Mix to a paste then add boiling water while stirring steadily, to make a cup, then add mashed ripe banana, lemon juice and cinnamon.

HEADACHES
Rosemary, basil or thyme oil rubbed into the forehead and temples can ease the pain.

Cayenne pepper comes from the dried, ground pods of red chillies (Capsicum species)

EYES, INFLAMED
Boil fennel leaves in water until liquid is reduced by half. Cool and apply to the eyes regularly in an eyebath. Make a fresh batch daily.

HICCUPS
Steep a few dill seeds in cold water for a few hours. Dill water is mild enough to use with children. Aniseed and fennel are also safe for children and can be steeped in the same way.

INDIGESTION
Peppermint tea is very soothing, especially after a big meal. Dill water, thyme tea, anise, caraway seeds and coriander seeds are also all effective. To eliminate flatulence, anise and angelica tea are the best cures.

Garlic (Allium sativum)

OBESITY
Many people are too fat because their livers cannot break down fatty foods efficiently. Dandelion coffee contains choline, a constituent of lecithin, which in turn helps break down these fatty foods, including cholesterol; so try changing your coffee drinking habits. Another way to cut down weight, is to chew fennel seeds whenever you feel the munchies coming on. They will allay your hunger and so help you regulate your meals and keep you on your diet. Parsley tea is an excellent drink for slimmers too, because it aids the removal of excess body fluids.

LIVER OR BLADDER TROUBLE
Parsley removes excess body fluids and is a general tonic for the digestive system. Also garlic corms, chives or chopped chervil leaves are all good blood purifiers.

NIGHTMARES AND SLEEPWALKING
Try catnip tea just before bed; excellent for children.

PERIOD PAINS
Valerian, chamomile and pennyroyal teas are all effective muscle relaxants that take the edge off the pain.

RHEUMATISM AND MUSCULAR PAIN
Dilute wintergreen oil (known as methylsalicilate in chemists) with a rubbing oil, such as almond or safflower, and massage into sore muscles. This should ease the pain. Undiluted wintergreen oil burns, so be careful. It has a very powerful, deep action and is able to unlock stiff muscles such as occur in sports injuries, sciatica, lumbago and fibrositis. It also smells rather strong. You may prefer to use rosemary oil, which calms the nerves as well as easing muscle pain. It is effective massaged into the back of the neck towards the scalp or on the brow and temples, if you have a headache or aching eyes. Lavender and marjoram oil are also considered effective for stiff muscles and rheumatic pain. For gout and rheumatism, a regular diet of chives and chervil is said to ease the pain.

ROUNDWORM
Southernwood tea is said to rid the body of roundworm.

SLEEPLESSNESS
There are several drinks and teas that are soothing and make sleep seem an attractive prospect. Dill water is one: steep a few dill seeds in boiling water for a couple of hours. A teaspoon of powdered valerian root stirred into milk and sweetened with a spoonful of honey is calming, and especially good if you are in pain or are traumatised. Chamomile tea makes a good late-night drink and should aid a good night's sleep.

SORE OR BLEEDING GUMS
Sage tea made with a couple of teaspoons of chopped leaves and 500 mL boiling water, left to stand for 10 minutes, should be helpful. Alternatively, just rub the gums with raw sage leaves.

TOOTHACHE
Chew marjoram leaves or put cloves to the aching area until you can reach a dentist.

PAMPER YOURSELF

Many herbs can be used for fragrance and beauty. Herbs have all sorts of efficacious qualities. By giving you good health, they automatically make you look better, but some herbs have particular attributes making them natural beauty preparations. Here are just a few of the more accessible and easily prepared treatments.

FOR YOUR BATH

Nothing is more beneficial to your sense of wellbeing than a warm bath at the end of the day. Add fresh herbs and you can make your bath as relaxing or as stimulating as you require.

If you prefer to give chemical proprietary deodorants a miss, you'll have to become a very regular bather. Take a shower or bath at least once a day. A handful of fresh lovage leaves sprinkled into your bath acts as an effective deodorant and is a more natural way to keep fresh. For a sweet-smelling bath that also has antiseptic, cleansing qualities, add a handful of yarrow leaves to the water.

Alternatively, make simple muslin or cheesecloth bags, fill with soothing herbs such as chamomile, peppermint, thyme or lavender, and hang them from the hot bath tap so hot water draws out the perfume.

A third method is to make an infusion of your favourite herb or mixed herbs, adding 1 litre of water. Steep for 2 hours and add to bath water.

However, the easiest and most aromatic way to enjoy a warm herb bath is with essential herb oils, available from health food shops. You only need a few drops.

Bath herbs make superb, inexpensive gifts, too. Choose herbs to suit the needs of the recipient. Here are the effects of some herbs in the bath:

- Dandelion, comfrey and nettle leaves make a good skin tonic and are invigorating.
- Chamomile flowers in a bath are most relaxing and good for the nerves. For oily skin, add yarrow leaves to the chamomile. Valerian root is another soothing herb for the bath.
- Lovage leaves have a cleansing effect in a warm, but not too hot, bath. If the user is prone to skin complaints, peppermint leaves mixed with horsetail are healing herbs in the bath.

A NATURAL DEODORANT
Lovage (*Levisticum officinale*)

In medieval times lovage was a popular herb for both medicinal and culinary use, but today it is less often found, despite its attractive yellow flowers and large decorative seed heads

Plant description: Hardy perennial, needing plenty of space. Very tall, to 2 m high, therefore best suited to the back of a border (quite unsuitable for container cultivation). Lovage likes a well-drained, rich, moist soil in a semi-shady position. You can sow seeds or propagate by root division in spring, but as lovage is one of the slowest herbs to germinate, you may prefer to buy a small plant.

Uses: Leaves are most generally used, chopped fresh or dried into soups, stews, salads and sauces, and the stems can be preserved as confectionery like angelica. Both stems and leaves have a celery-type flavour. If drying, only dry unblemished leaves. Lovage tea is said to be good for the digestion, for women's gynaecological problems, to relieve rheumatic pain and stimulate the kidneys, clearing the body of all its wastes. Lovage can also be used as a deodorant — just add a few leaves to your hot bath to release its cleansing properties.

Rosemary (Rosmarinus officinalis)

German chamomile (Matricaria chamomilla)

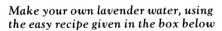
Make your own lavender water, using the easy recipe given in the box below

BATH HERBS

HERB	RELAXING	INVIGORATING	SWEET SCENT
Basil		X	
Comfrey		X	
Dandelion		X	
Geraniums — rose and lemon-scented	X		
Lavender	X		X
Lemon balm	X		
Lemon verbena			X
Mint			X
Peppermint		X	
Rosemary		X	
Thyme		X	
Violet			X

LAVENDER
English lavender — *Lavandula vera, L. officinalis* and *L. spica*
French lavender —*L. dentata*
Italian/Spanish lavender — *L. stoechas*

There are many kinds of lavender and many conflicting classifications, but lavenders all originate from moutainous areas of the Mediterranean.

Plant description: lavenders vary in height according to their species — anything from 30–90 cm, with pink, blue, green or white flowers. They all have silvery grey leaves which can be clipped to form a low hedge, as they were in Tudor knot gardens.

Grow from seed or take cuttings in spring or autumn and set them in sand. Pinch out plant centres to make them bushy, and prune plants down to the old wood in winter to keep well-shaped. Perennials, they last for many years with full sun, a poor but alkaline soil and no fertiliser.

Lavender has been widely used for cooking and in medicine in the past, but these days its aromatic leaves and flowers are mostly used in cosmetics. It is ideal for potpourri and can help repel moths in linen, carpets and clothes, wardrobes and chests.

Lavender oil is a distillation of French lavender flowers and leaves. Creams using this oil can relieve muscular stiffness and a cold compress applied to the forehead will temper a headache or giddiness.

Lavender water can be made by dropping a few drops of lavender oil into 600 mL chemist's alcohol with a lump of sugar. Shake well and transfer to an attractive bottle.

FOR YOUR HAIR

Many herbs can help to give you healthy, shiny hair. Make an infusion with for example, chamomile, nettle, parsley, rosemary, sage or yarrow and use as a daily rinse.

A few drops of rosemary oil in your last hair rinse strengthens, tones and stimulates hair roots to encourage growth. It is an excellent hair conditioner. You can also make a rosemary hair tonic by pouring a cupful of boiling water over a handful of rosemary leaves and leaving them to steep for a couple of hours. Use rosemary water, strained, as a last hair rinse. Pat your hair dry lightly if you want to maintain the rosemary perfume.

If you have blonde or fair hair, chamomile makes a great hair conditioner and maintains the blonde lights in your hair. Make an infusion by adding 500 mL boiling water to a handful of chamomile flowerheads. Leave them to stand for 20 minutes, strain and use as a final hair rinse.

Another hair conditioner is derived from marjoram. Make an infusion by simmering a couple of handfuls of marjoram leaves in 300 mL water for 5–10 minutes. Leave the infusion to cool, strain and apply to wet hair as a final hair rinse.

To darken greying hairs, make a sage infusion. Pour 500 mL boiling water onto a handful or more of sage leaves and allow to steep for at least 1 hour. Strain and apply as a last hair rinse, working the sage infusion well into the scalp. Save any of the infusion you can, and repeat two or three times more.

To make herbal shampoo, mix together 1 tablespoon mild soapflakes (e.g. Lux), 1 tablespoon borax, 30 g powdered chamomile flowers (or other herbs for hair already listed) and add 500 mL hot water. Beat together until the soap flakes are dissolved and bubbly. Wet hair with warm water and apply the shampoo, massaging it well into the scalp. Rinse, shampoo again and rinse out thoroughly.

Dry shampoo can be made by sprinkling orris root through your hair, without rubbing into the scalp. Leave for 10 minutes, then brush out thoroughly.

> **CONDITIONER**
> To extract herbal oil, bruise 2 tablespoons of your favourite herbs in a mincer or grinder. Pour into a bottle with 180 mL sunflower oil, and leave for 4 weeks in a sunny spot, remembering to shake the bottle daily.
>
> Strain, discard old herbs, and repeat the process for as many times as it takes for the oil to reach desired strength.
>
> Use as a hair conditioner: massage well into the scalp and leave on your hair for as long as possible, before rinsing out with a herbal rinse, such as a chamomile or sage infusion.
>
> Suitable herbs include chamomile, nettle, parsley, rosemary and sage, all of which are generally good for the hair.

Lavender has many uses: for bouquets, sachets, potpourri, soothing oil and cleansing water

COOKING WITH HERBS — AN A TO Z GUIDE

These days, the emphasis is on light, healthy meals, using the freshest ingredients in luscious combinations. With dieticians and doctors recommending us to drastically reduce salt intake and avoid heart attack, one way to make food tasty and add to its health-giving properties, is to start cooking with herbs on a regular basis.

In this section, we list the most popular herbs, with details on how to use them. All are readily available from fruit markets and green-grocers. They are also easy to grow in your own garden.

Fresh is always best, but if something is out of season, substitute dried. The ratio is usually 1:4, for example, 1 teaspoon dried oregano to 1 tablespoon fresh. Sometimes a recipe will specify more of the dried herb, for a stronger and more pungent flavour. Experiment, using small quantities at first, until you find out what suits your palate best.

Herbs can play an important part in any dish. They are used to add flavour, texture and decoration. The appearance and nature of a salad, for example, can be changed simply by varying the kinds of herbs added, or the flavour of oil or vinegar used.

> **MEASUREMENTS**
> Standard metric measurements are used throughout the following recipes.
> 1 teaspoon = 5 mL
> 1 tablespoon = 20 mL
> 1 cup = 250 mL
> All measurements are level.

BASIL

BUSH BASIL (Ocimum minimum)
SWEET BASIL (O. basilicum))

Plant description: *Of the 40 odd types of the annual herb basil, sweet and bush basil are the most common and the easiest to grow. Bush basil grows only 15 cm high. Sweet is taller at 60 cm, has the larger leaves and is more flavoursome.*

Basil originates from India and likes a sunny but sheltered position. Water in the heat of the day — the leaves as well as the roots like moisture. Pinch out the centres to make the plants bushy and watch out for snails and slugs.

Uses: *Dried basil leaves were once used in snuff to relieve nervous headaches and aid digestion, but the leaves do not store well. These days, basil is reknowned as the main ingredient in pesto. It tastes wonderful with tomatoes and goes well with eggs, mushrooms, pasta and in green salads.*

Sweet basil (Ocimum basilicum)

Fillets of Sole with Zucchini and Basil

350 g zucchini, sliced
1 tablespoon oil
1 sprig rosemary
12 leaves fresh basil
salt and freshly ground black pepper
150 g tomatoes, peeled and chopped
a little plain flour
8 fillets of sole (or other white-fleshed fish)
80 g butter
breadcrumbs
1 lemon

Fry zucchini in a little oil with rosemary, basil, salt and pepper. When nearly done, add tomatoes and fry for a further 2 minutes. Flour sole fillets and brown in butter. Butter an ovenproof dish and arrange fillets in one row if possible. Cover with zucchini-tomato mixture, sprinkle with breadcrumbs, dot with butter and put in the oven at 225°C (430°F) for 5–10 minutes until brown. Serve decorated with basil leaves and lemon wedges or slices.
Serves 4

FREEZING HERBS
You can deep freeze some herbs, like fennel, basil, sorrel, tarragon and mint. Blanch them in boiling water then plunge them into icy water for a minute. Pat dry, put them into freezer bags, remove excess air, seal, label and date.

Pesto

If you like the flavour of basil then you will probably already know this sauce. It has to be one of the great flavour combinations in the world. Serve spooned through freshly cooked pasta. The sauce will keep well if refrigerated in a jar with a good layer of olive oil. Pour off the oil (reserving for another use), bring back to room temperature and stir the sauce when ready to use.

1 large bunch fresh basil leaves
1 large bunch fresh parsley leaves
4 cloves garlic, peeled
3 tablespoons pine nuts
1 teaspoon salt
freshly ground black pepper
⅓ cup grated Parmesan cheese (40 g)
¾–1 cup olive oil (180–250 mL)

Blend basil, parsley and garlic in a blender or food processor until finely chopped. Add pine nuts, salt, pepper and Parmesan. Blend until a smooth paste is formed. With motor still running, add oil in a slow, steady stream until the mixture becomes a smooth sauce. Do not cook the sauce for it will separate, and use spooned over hot pasta, gnocchi, jacket-baked potatoes or stirred into a minestrone-style soup.
Makes about 2 cups (500 mL)

Fresh Herb Fettuccine with Smoked Salmon and Asparagus

Pasta flavoured with fresh herbs makes a wonderful base for light, fresh sauces. Herbs and vegetables which are in season at the same time, like the basil and asparagus in the recipe, often make perfect partners and require little else to flavour the dish. Along with the taste, the attractive appearance of green herbs through the pasta is reason enough to serve it with just melted butter and grated cheese.

Try basil pasta with a cold sauce made from fresh ripe tomatoes, or fettuccine flavoured with fresh sage and coated with a creamy Gorgonzola sauce.

PASTA
300 g plain flour or 150 g flour and 150 g semolina
pinch salt
2 teaspoons finely chopped fresh parsley
2 teaspoons finely chopped fresh basil
2 eggs

SAUCE
350 g fresh asparagus spears, trimmed, peeled and halved
30 g butter
150 g sliced smoked salmon, cut into strips
1 cup cream (250 mL)
freshly ground black pepper

To make the pasta, pile flour and salt on a work surface and make a well in the middle. Add herbs and eggs and begin to incorporate into the flour, using a fork. When you have a loosely coherent dough, use your hands and knead it, adding a little flour or water if necessary for it to become smooth and elastic. Knead for at least 6 minutes and then rest, covered with plastic or a damp cloth, for 30 minutes.

Divide the dough in two and roll each half out into a thin, even sheet using a rolling pin or a hand-cranked pasta machine. Rest again, covered, for 10 minutes before cutting the sheets into long thin fettuccine strips. Set aside but only cover if you feel the pasta will crack before cooking it.

In a large saucepan of boiling water put the bottom halves of the asparagus; boil for a minute before adding the tops and continue to cook until tender. Remove with a slotted spoon and rinse under cold water. Drain, and when cool enough to handle, cut each half into halves again, discarding any woody sections. Top up the pan of water and bring back to the boil. Begin cooking the fettuccine.

In a large frying pan melt butter and add smoked salmon. Saute gently for 30 seconds before adding cream. Increase the heat a little and cook to thicken, then add black pepper generously and toss in the asparagus.

When the pasta is *al dente*, drain and transfer to the pan with the sauce. Toss through, then serve with freshly grated Parmesan and the pepper mill handed around the table.

Serves 4 as an entree, 2–3 as a luncheon or supper dish

Basil and Pasta Salad with ingredients for making Pesto

Basil and Pasta Salad

185 g corkscrew pasta (spirelli)
salt
¼ green cabbage, finely shredded
6 radishes, thinly sliced
1 small green capsicum, seeded and thinly sliced
1 punnet cherry tomatoes, halved if large   (250 g)
½ telegraph cucumber, thinly sliced
1 ripe avocado, peeled and sliced
½ bunch chives and extra basil leaves to garnish

DRESSING
2 bunches fresh basil
4 cloves garlic, peeled
2 teaspoons Dijon-style mustard
juice ½ lemon
¾ cup olive oil (180 mL)
salt and freshly ground black pepper

Cook pasta in boiling salted water until *al dente*. Drain and cool. Prepare the vegetables.

To make dressing, wash basil and strip leaves from stalks (reserve a few for garnish). Place leaves in the container of a food processor with garlic, mustard and half the lemon juice. Blend until finely chopped. Slowly add oil to the container with the motor still running and process until dressing thickens. Season well and add remaining lemon juice to taste.

Toss all salad ingredients together in a bowl with dressing. Snip over chives and garnish with reserved basil leaves.

Serves 6

Baby Carrots with Fresh Basil

500 g baby carrots
2 tablespoons finely chopped fresh basil
40 g butter

Place carrots in a saucepan and just cover with boiling water. Cover pan, bring to the boil and cook for 10 minutes. Drain, toss well with basil, add butter and return to the heat. Allow the butter to melt, mixing well with the carrots.

Serves 6

Bay leaves (Laurus nobilis)

BAY

(LAURUS NOBILIS)

Plant description: *Bay is a perennial evergreen tree, not a herb strictly speaking. It can grow 11 m high but is usually cultivated as either a formal standard shrub in a tub or a low hedge. It has tough, shiny aromatic leaves, small yellowy white flowers and purplish fruits. Bay trees like a sunny position, although they will tolerate a little shade. Not frost resistant, they are otherwise quite easy to grow and can be clipped. Propagate from seed or from 20 cm cuttings in late summer. They grow slowly and cuttings may take six months to root. Never let them dry out and fertilise occasionally.*

Uses: *Bay leaves can be picked and dried out any time. They are used as part of the bouquet garni to flavour soups, stews and casseroles; or with poached fish, milk puddings, bread sauce and in marinades. Medicinally bay oil can be used to relieve rheumatism or skin conditions.*

Beef in Red Wine

2 tablespoons olive oil
1.25 kg chuck or gravy beef, trimmed
  and cut into 3 cm cubes
3 tablespoons plain flour
2 cups red wine (500 mL)
1 cup water (250 mL)
bouquet garni
salt and freshly ground black pepper
60 g butter
500 g pickling onions, trimmed
250 g button mushrooms, stalks
  trimmed

Heat oil in a heavy flameproof casserole. Brown beef well a few pieces at a time. Return all meat to the pan and add flour, scraping in all the pan juices and crusty bits. Pour over wine and water. Add bouquet garni and season well. Bring to the boil. Cover and place casserole in a 150°C (300°F) oven for 1½ hours.

Half an hour before end of cooking time, melt half the butter in a heavy-based frying pan and brown the onions until golden. Set aside. Melt remaining butter and saute the mushrooms quickly. Add onions and mushrooms to beef and stir through. Continue cooking for a further half an hour or until meat is tender. Remove bouquet garni before serving. Serve hot with creamy mashed potatoes.
  Serves 4–6

Duck and Chicken Liver Pate

250 g duck or turkey livers
250 g chicken livers
1 large onion
2 cloves garlic, crushed
250 g unsalted butter
3 tablespoons chopped mixed fresh
  sage or marjoram, parsley and chives
salt and freshly ground black pepper
2 tablespoons Grand Marnier
fresh bay leaves
90 g clarified butter, melted

Remove any fibres from livers. Chop onion and crush garlic with a large pinch salt. Melt 60 g butter in a heavy-based frying pan and saute onions and garlic until soft. Remove with a slotted spoon to a bowl.

In the same pan, saute livers briefly, a few at a time, leaving them quite pink inside. Combine with onion in the bowl of a food processor and blend until smooth; cool.

Cream remaining butter until smooth and combine with liver mixture and chopped herbs. Season well and stir in Grand Marnier.

Pour into a terrine or serving dish. Leave to set slightly. Place a fresh bay leaf or two on the surface and spoon over melted clarified butter. Refrigerate until set. Serve with Melba toast or chunks of crusty bread.
  Serves 6–8 as an entree

Herbed Tomato Sauce

¼ cup olive oil (60 mL)
1 onion, finely chopped
2 cloves garlic, crushed
1 kg ripe tomatoes, peeled, seeded and
  finely chopped
3 bay leaves
2½ teaspoons sugar
2 teaspoons finely chopped basil or
  1 teaspoon dried basil
2 teaspoons finely chopped oregano or
  1 teaspoon dried oregano
½ cup dry white wine (125 mL)

Heat oil and fry onion for 5 minutes. Add garlic and fry a further 2 minutes. Add remaining ingredients and simmer, stirring occasionally for 1 hour or until thickened.

Note: Herbed Tomato Sauce will keep up to 5 days refrigerated or may be frozen.

Makes approximately 2¾ cups (700 mL)

Duck and Chicken Liver Pate served with crusty bread

CARAWAY

(CARUM CARVI)

Plant description: *This attractive biennial is valuable for its seeds. It grows 60 cm high, has soft, feathery foliage and white flowers in summer. Caraway germinates quickly from seeds. Plant straight into the soil, choosing a sunny position in a well-drained spot. Remove seeds when brown and finish the drying process indoors. This herb can also be grown in a container despite its considerable root, which can be cooked like carrots.*

Uses: *Caraway seeds improve the flavour and aid the digestion of cabbage, parsnips, turnips, baked apples and pears. Oils from the aromatic seeds also help the digestive system assimilate starchy foods such as bread, pasta and biscuits.*

Above: Leaves and seeds of the caraway plant (Carum carvi)
Below: Caraway Seed Biscuits and Caraway Seed Cake

Caraway Seed Biscuits

Store these crisp biscuits in an airtight tin, after cooling.

¾ cup plain flour (90 g)
¼ cup self-raising flour (30 g)
¼ cup cornflour (30 g)
pinch salt
pinch cayenne or chilli powder
125 g butter
1 teaspoon caraway seeds
1 cup grated Cheddar cheese (125 g)
¼ cup grated Parmesan cheese (30 g)
extra caraway or sesame seeds, to sprinkle

Sift flours together with salt and cayenne into a bowl. Rub in butter until mixture resembles fine breadcrumbs. Add caraway seeds. Stir cheese into the mixture using a knife until mixture gathers until into a ball.

Pinch off walnut-sized pieces of dough and roll into balls. Place on greased baking trays and press out lightly using the back of a fork. Sprinkle with extra caraway seeds and bake in a 180°C (350°F) oven for 12–15 minutes, or until golden brown. Cool on a wire rack and store in an airtight tin.

Makes 30

Caraway Seed Cake

2 cups plain flour (250 g)
2 teaspoons nutmeg
1 teaspoon bicarbonate of soda
1 teaspoon baking powder
125 g butter
1 teaspoon vanilla
1 cup caster sugar (220 g)
½ cup brown sugar (85 g)
3 eggs
1 teaspoon caraway seeds
½ cup milk (125 mL), soured with 1
    teaspoon lemon juice

TOPPING
⅓ cup sugar (80 g)
1½ teaspoons cinnamon
2 teaspoons grated orange rind
¾ cup soft breadcrumbs (45 g)
40 g butter, melted

Preheat oven to 200°C (400°F). Sift flour, nutmeg, bicarbonate and baking powder twice. Cream butter, vanilla and sugars until light and fluffy. Beat in eggs. Fold in flour mixture and caraway seeds alternately with sour milk. Place mixture into a 20 cm greased and lined cake tin.

Bake for 35–40 minutes. Halfway through cooking time, sprinkle over combined topping ingredients and return to oven. Test with a skewer for doneness. Cool on a cake rack and serve.

Caraway Soup

60 g butter
3 tablespoons plain flour
1 teaspoon caraway seeds
2.5 litres beef stock
1 rasher bacon
1 egg yolk
½ cup sour cream (125 mL)

In a pan, heat butter until sizzling. Stir in flour to combine. Add caraway seeds and stock, and bring to the boil. Add bacon, lower heat and simmer 30 minutes. Combine egg yolk and cream in a soup tureen. Strain in soup and serve.

Serves 6

CHIVES

(ALLIUM SCHOENOPRASUM)

Plant description: *Chives belong to the same genus as garlic and have many similar medicinal powers. Grassy-leaved perennials, they produce pinky mauve pompom flowers in spring. Plant them in a rich soil and give plenty of water during dry periods. Easy to grow from seed, they reach about 20 cm, and make an attractive border plant. Snip frequently to make the plants bushy and remove flowers to gain maximum flavour from the leaves. As they prefer semi-shade in summer and full sun in winter, a spot beneath a deciduous tree is ideal for planting.*

Uses: *Chives contain iron, pectin, sulphur and a mild, natural antibiotic. They help break down fatty foods, making them a useful herb to sufferers of high blood pressure. They are said to stimulate the appetite, hasten recuperation, ease the pain of rheumatism and gout, and cleanse the kidneys. Their chopped, hollow leaves are tasty in omelettes, salads, soups, mayonnaise, cream cheese and many other dishes.*

Chives (Allium schoenoprasum)

Scallop Bundles with Herb Cream Sauce

500 g scallops
1 leek, sliced and rinsed
few peppercorns
pinch salt
bouquet garni
½ cup dry white wine (125 mL)
1 cup water (250 mL)
½ bunch chives, snipped
grated rind ½ lemon
1 teaspoon black sesame seeds
8 sheets filo pastry
60 g butter, melted

HERB CREAM
⅔ cup poaching liquid (180 mL)
1 cup creme fraiche (250 mL)
salt and freshly ground black pepper
3 fresh sorrel leaves

Trim veins from scallops. Place sliced leek in a large saucepan with peppercorns, salt, bouquet garni, white wine and water. Bring to the boil and add scallops. Lower heat and poach gently for 2 minutes. Leave to cool in the liquid. Drain well, reserving all poaching liquid for the sauce. Toss the scallops with chives, lemon rind and sesame seeds.

Take a sheet of filo pastry and brush liberally with melted butter. Cut into quarters and lay the four squares one on top of the other. Spoon a tablespoon of the scallop filling onto the centre of the pastry and fold into a parcel. Secure the top with a soft piece of string. Repeat with remaining pastry and scallop mixture. Place on a greased baking tray and bake in a 190°C (375°F) oven for 12–15 minutes or until golden and crisp. Remove string and tie with a plain chive.

To make the sauce, reduce reserved poaching liquid to ⅔ cup by boiling rapidly. Strain into a measuring cup. Place creme fraiche and poaching liquid into a small saucepan. Bring to the boil and season. Cut the sorrel leaves into strips and add to the sauce just before serving. Serve each individual plate with two scallop bundles sitting in a pool of hot sauce.

Serves 2 as an entree

Creme Fraiche

Creme Fraiche now appears much more often in recipes and on menus. The tangy flavour of this cream is excellent. It can be used to make a light savoury sauce or sweetened with a scented or vanilla sugar, brown sugar or a liqueur and beaten until thick. Serve with fresh or poached fruit. The beauty of the cream is that it will keep for up to two weeks in the refrigerator, so you can always have it on hand.

300 mL fresh cream
200 mL natural (unflavoured) low-fat yoghurt

Beat cream and yoghurt together in a small bowl or jar. Cover and refrigerate overnight. Use as required.
Makes 2 cups (500 mL)

Carrot and Chive Salad

4 carrots
2 bunches chives, snipped
½ bunch shallots, slivered
½ cup sultanas (90 g)

HERB VINAIGRETTE
1 tablespoon Dijon-style mustard
1½ tablespoons white wine vinegar
1½ tablespoons chopped fresh herbs
e.g. parsley, chives or thyme
90 mL olive oil
salt and freshly ground black pepper

Peel carrots and grate finely into a bowl. Combine with chives, shallots and sultanas. To make vinaigrette, place mustard in a bowl. Whisk in vinegar and herbs. Gradually whisk in oil until mixture thickens. Season to taste and pour over salad.
Serves 4

> **INDOOR HERBS**
> **Once established, rosemary, sage, marjoram, mint and chives will grow indoors quite happily.**

Salmon and Chive Log

420 g canned red salmon
200 g cream cheese, at room
  temperature
2 tablespoons sour cream
1 tablespoon lemon juice
1 bunch shallots, chopped
2 bunches chives, snipped
freshly ground black pepper
⅓ cup walnut or pecan pieces (40 g)

Drain salmon and remove any skin and bones. Flake into large pieces. Beat cream cheese, sour cream and lemon juice together until smooth, but still firm. Add shallots, a quarter of the chives and season with pepper. Fold through nuts and salmon. If the mixture is very soft, chill until firm enough to handle.

Place salmon mixture onto a sheet of plastic wrap or greaseproof paper. Roll up into a log. Chill until quite firm. Place the remaining snipped chives on a clean sheet of greaseproof paper. Unwrap the salmon log and roll in the chives to evenly coat. Serve with crackers and crisp vegetables. Alternatively, spoon the mixture into a serving bowl and cover the surface with snipped chives.

  Serves 4–6

Sesame Cheese Pie

500 g ricotta cheese
300 mL sour cream
2 eggs
100 g grated Cheddar cheese
½ bunch shallots, chopped
3 tablespoons chopped fresh mint
1 bunch snipped chives
375 g shortcrust or puff pastry
1 extra egg, beaten
2 tablespoons sesame seeds, for
  decoration

Crumble cheese into a large bowl. Beat in sour cream and eggs. Stir through Cheddar, shallots, mint and chives.

Cut pastry in half and roll out one half on a lightly floured surface to form a rectangle 18 cm x 33 cm. Set on a greased baking tray. Spoon filling over the pastry, leaving a 3cm border. Brush edges with water. Roll out remaining pastry to a rectangle slightly larger than the first and cover filling, pressing edges together to seal. Roll edge and score with the back of a knife. Make a few slits in the top to allow steam to escape. Brush pie with beaten egg and sprinkle with sesame seeds.

Bake in a 190°C (375°F) oven for 25–35 minutes or until golden brown. Serve hot with a crisp green salad.

  Serves 6

Souffle Potatoes

4 large old potatoes
1 cup grated Cheddar cheese (125 g)
freshly ground black pepper
4 tablespoons sour cream
1 tablespoon chopped chives
1 tablespoon chopped fresh parsley
pinch paprika
2 egg yolks
3 egg whites

Wash potatoes, pierce with a skewer in several places and bake at 180°C (350°F) for 1–1½ hours. The potatoes should be cooked but still intact. Cut a lid off each potato and scoop out the centre, leaving some of the flesh around the skin to form a casing.

Mash potato with all remaining ingredients except egg whites. Beat egg whites until stiff and gently fold into potato mixture. Spoon into potato cases and place them on an oven tray. Bake at 200°C (400°F) until the tops are golden brown and puffy.

  Serves 4

CORIANDER

(CORIANDRUM SATIVUM))

Plant description: *Coriander is an annual grown for its aromatic seeds and leaves. It can reach 60 cm in height. It likes light, rich and well-drained soil in open sun. When growing, it can smell rather unpleasant, so do not attempt to grow it indoors: more established plants develop a quite pleasant aroma.*

Sow the seeds in early spring where they are to grow, preferably close to dill, fennel and chervil. The herb will grow with feathery leaves and delicate umbelliferous mauve flowers to about 80 cm. When the seeds have turned brown, harvest the old flower heads carefully and complete the drying process indoors. The seeds remain fertile for about five years.

Uses: *Coriander seeds are good for the digestion, helping carbohydrates to break down in the body. The seeds are indispensible for curries and pickled fruit. Whole or ground they also complement fish, baked or stewed fruit, cauliflower, beetroot and celery. Coriander leaves are tasty in salads and soups, and the entire plant is used in Thai cuisine.*

Coriander leaves and root (Coriander sativum)

Coriander and Pear Salad

The flavour of coriander and pear is delightful. A few pecan or walnuts may be added to give this salad an extra nutty crunch.

4 large ripe pears
1 bunch watercress
1 punnet pear or cherry tomatoes (250 g)
6 tablespoons fresh coriander leaves
½ bunch shallots, slivered
½ bunch chives, snipped

DRESSING
2 teaspoons Dijon-style mustard
2–3 tablespoons lemon juice
½ cup olive oil (125 mL)
1 clove garlic, crushed with a pinch salt
freshly ground black pepper

Peel pears, halve and core. Slice lengthways and arrange in a salad bowl lined with watercress. Scatter over tomatoes, coriander, shallots and chives.

To make dressing, place all ingredients in a small bowl. Whisk together until combined. Pour over salad and lightly toss just before serving.
Serves 4

Baked Snapper with a Citrus and Coriander Sauce

200 g penne pasta
½ cup vegetable oil (125 mL)
4 small-medium snapper steaks or other white fleshed fish, trimmed
2–3 cloves garlic, crushed
1 tablespoon chopped fresh coriander, and some sprigs for decoration
160 mL tomato puree or juice from canned, peeled tomatoes
3 tablespoons fresh citrus juice: lime, lemon, Seville orange or a combination
chilli flakes, to taste

Cook penne in boiling salted water until barely *al dente*. Drain, and stir through a little vegetable oil to prevent sticking. Transfer to an ovenproof dish.

In a pan heat some of the oil and brown the snapper on both sides. Transfer to the dish and lay side by side on top of the penne, covering it completely.

Heat remaining oil in pan and gently fry garlic. Add chopped coriander, tomato puree and citrus juice. Cook, stirring, until the sauce boils and gives off a citrus aroma. Sprinkle in chilli flakes to taste, then pour sauce over snapper. Pour in a

little water, perhaps ¼ cup (60 mL), to make sure all the pasta is moistened. Cover loosely with foil and bake at 220°C (425°F), for 25–30 minutes, or until the snapper is tender. Decorate with coriander sprigs and serve from the dish.
Serves 4

Thai Chicken Salad

4–6 boneless chicken breasts
¼ cup rice wine vinegar (60 mL)
1 tablespoon light soy sauce
1 tablespoon raw sugar
2 tablespoons fresh coriander leaves
1 tablespoon sesame seed oil

SALAD VEGETABLES
1 red and 1 green capsicum, seeded and finely sliced
½ bunch shallots, finely sliced on the diagonal
1 large carrot, julienned
½ telegraph cucumber, peeled and julienned
2 tomatoes, peeled, seeded and cut into eighths
1 small head cos lettuce

DRESSING
3 tablespoons rice wine vinegar
1 tablespoon Japanese horseradish paste or chopped horseradish
1 teaspoon sugar
freshly ground black pepper
3 tablespoons walnut oil

GARNISH
3 tablespoons each coriander, mint and basil
½ bunch chives
2 tablespoons sesame seed, toasted

Cut each chicken breast into three long strips. Place in a glass or ceramic bowl and add vinegar, soy sauce, sugar and coriander. Toss to combine, cover and refrigerate overnight.

Heat sesame oil in a wok and stir-fry chicken pieces over high heat until just cooked. Turn out onto a plate and prepare salad vegetables.

To make the dressing, combine first four ingredients in a bowl. Whisk in oil until combined.

Toss vegetables together with half the dressing. Arrange in the centre of each individual plate with a few small cos leaves. Divide chicken strips between the plates, arranging them over the salad. Sprinkle each plate with a little more dressing and garnish each with fresh herbs and toasted sesame seeds.
Serves 4–6

Thai Chicken Salad

Spring Salad with Coriander Dressing

Coriander gives a wonderful oriental flavour to any ingredient it is added to. When this slightly sweet dressing is used over a fruit based salad, such as pears or mangoes with the addition of spring onions or shallots, the combination is magical.

SALAD
1 small mignonette lettuce
1 witloof
100 g rocket leaves (type of lettuce)
1 small bunch watercress
2 small radicchios
8 small nasturtium leaves
3 tablespoons chervil sprigs
3 tablespoons young flat-leaf parsley
 sprigs
1 green capsicum
½ punnet cherry or pear tomatoes
 (125 g)
½ bunch shallots, slivered

CORIANDER DRESSING
2 teaspoons Dijon-style mustard
3 tablespoons lemon juice
6–8 tablespoons olive oil
salt and freshly ground black pepper
1 teaspoon sugar
2 tablespoons chopped fresh coriander

Wash and dry mignonette lettuce, witloof, rocket, watercress, radicchio, nasturtium leaves and herb sprigs. Arrange in a salad bowl. Slice capsicum thinly and add to salad with tomatoes and shallots.

To make dressing, place mustard in a small bowl with lemon juice. Whisk in oil until mixture thickens. Season well with salt, pepper and sugar. Stir through coriander. Toss salad with dressing just before serving.
Serves 4–6

Coriander Sambal

3 tablespoons chopped fresh coriander
2 teaspoons raw sugar
2 tablespoons rice wine vinegar
1 tablespoon hot water

Place coriander in a small bowl. Add raw sugar, vinegar and hot water. Stir until sugar has dissolved. Cool and serve with prawns, barbecued meats or satays.
Makes ½ cup (125 mL)

DILL

(ANETHUM GRAVEOLENS)

Plant description: *Dill is a fast-growing annual with fern-like, delicate leaves, attractive yellow flowers and aromatic seeds. Easy to grow, it is often self-seeding. Collected seeds retain their fertility for at least 10 years. It likes a sunny position, growing to 90 cm in warm climates. Sow in the place you intend to grow the herb, away from angelica and fennel.*

Uses: *Dill seeds and leaves can both be eaten. They contain potassium, sodium, sulphur and phosphorus and have a slightly astringent, metallic flavour. They go well with potatoes, cheese and salads, and in white sauces, egg and seafood dishes, and soups. Dill seeds also improve the flavour of pickles.*

Dill has a reputation for relieving indigestion. It is mild enough to be administered to colicky babies as a tea. Dill water, available from chemists, has long been used as a sedative for young children.

Dill leaves (Anethum graveolens)

Gravalax

This is a delicious and interesting way to serve fresh salmon. The curing process takes two days but Gravalax may be kept for up to a week in the refrigerator. Serve very thinly sliced, as you would smoked salmon. Another way to serve this is to cut the Gravalax slices into thin strips, and toss together with julienned strips of cucumber and a light dressing.

half side of salmon (500–750 g)
½ cup rock salt (125 g)
½ cup sugar (125 g)
⅔ bunch snipped fresh dill
¼ cup freshly ground black pepper

Remove any bones from the salmon, using a pair of pliers. Mix rock salt, sugar, dill and pepper in a bowl together. Lay salmon flesh side up on a large sheet of aluminium foil. Spread dill mixture over to cover surface.

Wrap salmon securely in the foil and set on a tray to catch any juices that might run. Cover with a teatowel and arrange weights on top of fish. Marinate in the refrigerator for two days. To serve, scrape off most of the dill mixture and slice very thinly. Serve with wedges of lemon.
Serves 4

Marinara Salad

WARM DRESSING
2 cloves garlic, crushed
1 teaspoon salt
6 tablespoons chopped fresh parsley
1 bunch fresh dill, chopped
2 tablespoons grated Parmesan cheese
½ cup stock made with 2 chicken cubes (125 mL)
½ cup oil (125 mL)
juice 1 lemon and grated rind ½ lemon

SALAD
2 tablespoons oil
1 bunch shallots, peeled and thinly sliced
2 cloves garlic, finely chopped
2 cups fish stock (500 mL)
500 g scallops
500 g uncooked peeled prawns (heads removed)
2 large carrots, julienned
1 litre water
juice 1 lemon
1 teaspoon salt
6 tablespoons chopped fresh dill
freshly ground black pepper
500 g conchiglie rigate (shell-shaped pasta)

Combine dressing ingredients, mix well and set aside in a small saucepan.

To make salad, heat oil and saute shallots and garlic until softened. Add fish stock. Reduce heat, add scallops and poach for 1–2 minutes only. Remove with slotted spoon and keep warm. Add prawns to stock and remove as soon as they turn opaque. Add to reserved scallops. Do not overcook as both will shrink and lose their taste. Increase heat to reduce stock to approximately half quantity. Add all remaining ingredients.

To assemble, cook pasta until *al dente*, drain well. Heat dressing, pour over pasta and mix well. Serve pasta topped with seafood mixture at room temperature.
Serves 8

Dill-Mustard Potato Salad

2 litres chicken stock
1 kg tiny new baby potatoes, unpeeled
¾ cup vegetable oil (180 mL)
1 egg, room temperature
3 tablespoons Dijon-style mustard
2 tablespoons finely chopped fresh dill or 2 teaspoons dried dill
1 teaspoon red wine vinegar
1 teaspoon lemon juice
freshly ground black pepper
½ cup sour cream (125 mL)
3 celery stalks, thinly sliced
1 onion, thinly sliced
½ bunch chives, snipped

Combine stock and potatoes and bring to boil over high heat. Reduce heat and cook potatoes just until tender. Drain immediately and rinse with cold water to cool. Drain potatoes well.

In a food processor or blender combine 3 tablespoons oil, the egg, mustard, dill, vinegar, lemon juice and pepper and blend until mixture is slightly thickened, about 10 seconds. With machine running, slowly pour remaining oil through feed tube in thin, steady stream and mix well. Add sour cream and blend 3 seconds to combine.

Slice potatoes into quarters and combine in a salad bowl with celery and onion. Pour over the dressing and fold through the salad. Cover and refrigerate until ready to serve. Garnish with chives.
Serves 6

Dill-Mustard Potato Salad

Flathead and Dill Parcels with Dill Sauce

8 small fillets flathead (or other white-fleshed fish)
8 English spinach leaves, blanched and stems removed
grated rind 1 lemon
freshly ground black pepper
¼ telegraph cucumber, julienned
1 carrot, peeled and julienned
1 bunch fresh dill
30 g firm butter
8 sheets filo pastry
155 g unsalted butter, melted

DILL SAUCE
3 egg yolks
juice ½ lemon
salt and pepper
185 g unsalted butter
2 tablespoons chopped fresh dill

Remove skin and any bones from fillet. Place each fillet on a blanched spinach leaf. Sprinkle with lemon rind and black pepper. Arrange strips of cucumber and carrot, and a sprig of dill over each fillet. Cut butter into 8 slivers. Place a sliver on each fillet. Wrap up each fish with its spinach leaf, tucking the thin tail end up inside.

Brush a sheet of pastry with melted butter. Place a fish bundle at the end of the sheet and wrap up like a parcel. Set on a greased baking tray and brush with melted butter. Repeat with remaining fillets and pastry. Bake in a 190°C (375°F) for 12–15 minutes or until golden brown. Serve hot with sauce.

To make sauce, place egg yolks in the container of a food processor with 1 tablespoon lemon juice. Season with salt and pepper. Melt butter until foaming. With the motor running, pour in the sizzling butter, slowly at first, until a thick sauce forms. Add remaining lemon juice and stir through dill. Spoon into a deep serving bowl. Serve warm.

Note: To keep warm, place sauce bowl over a pan of hot water, and stir often. Cover closely with plastic wrap to prevent sauce from forming a skin.

Serves 8

Baby Squash with Dill

500 g miniature squash or zucchini, topped and tailed
60 g butter
1 cup water (250 mL)
freshly ground black pepper
1 tablespoon finely chopped fresh dill
juice ½ lemon
extra fresh dill, to garnish

Place squash in a heavy-based saucepan with butter and water. Season with pepper. Cover pan and bring to the boil, then reduce heat and simmer for 5 minutes.

Add dill and lemon juice, and boil, uncovered, until the liquid has almost evaporated. Serve squash immediately garnished with dill.

Serves 4–6

Flathead and Dill Parcels with Dill Sauce, and Baby Squash with Dill

FENNEL RED, SWEET OR GARDEN

(FOENICULUM VULGARE)

Plant description: *Not to be confused with the vegetable that you eat cooked or in salads (Florence fennel, F. dulce), the herb fennel is a fast-growing perennial found in waste ground all over the world. With attractive feathery leaves and pretty yellow flowers, it will grow to a height of 1.5 m in full sun, and will produce more leaves if trimmed. Plant away from dill, coriander or caraway to avoid cross-pollination.*

Uses: *Fennel leaves are used to flavour and garnish many dishes, particularly fish. Gather the seeds when dark brown, and sprinkle into bread dough, cakes, pumpkin soup, borscht or cottage cheese; or try cooking them with oily fish. Chewing seeds can also be useful to stave off hunger if you're slimming, or to vaporise mucus if you have a cold. Fennel is also used to strengthen eyesight.*

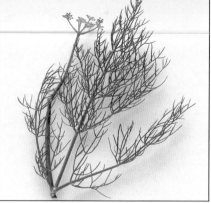

Above: Fennel (Foeniculum vulgare)

Mussels with Fennel

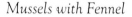

1 kg fresh mussels
few sprigs fresh fennel
1¼ cup dry white wine (310 mL)
½ cup water (125 mL)
bouquet garni
salt and freshly ground black pepper
6 shallots, chopped
30 g butter
2 tablespoons plain flour

Scrub and rinse mussels and remove the hairy beard using a sharp knife. Discard any mussels that are not firmly closed.

Place fennel, wine, water, bouquet garni, salt, pepper and shallots in a large saucepan. Bring to the boil and add prepared mussels. Cook covered for 3–4 minutes or until all mussels have opened. Strain, and reserve cooking liquid, discarding bouquet garni. Place mussels in serving bowls and keep warm while making sauce.

Melt butter in rinsed out pan and add flour. Cook over moderate heat, stirring for a minute. Pour over the reserved cooking liquid, whisking constantly, and cook until sauce has slightly thickened. Spoon over mussels and serve at once garnished with fennel.

Serves 4

Fennel Sauce

Serve warm with poached or baked salmon. Also delicious served over poached chicken.

185 g unsalted butter
3 egg yolks
juice ½ lemon
salt and freshly ground black pepper
2 tablespoons chopped fresh fennel
4 tablespoons creme fraiche

Melt butter in a small saucepan until foaming. Place egg yolks in the container of a food processor and add 1 tablespoon lemon juice; season. With the motor running slowly, add foaming butter in a slow steady stream, until sauce thickens. Stir through chopped fennel. Add remaining lemon juice to taste. Stir through creme fraiche and serve warm.

Makes 1 cup (250 mL)

Fish Barbecued with Fennel

Fish Barbecued with Fennel

4 medium-sized, white-fleshed whole fish
large bunch fennel

MARINADE
½ cup olive oil (125 mL)
juice 1 lemon
4 tablespoons Cognac or brandy
salt and freshly ground black pepper
2 cloves garlic, crushed

Scale, gut and clean fish. Place one fennel branch inside each fish. Score fish with 3 x 5 cm long incisions in each side.

Combine marinade ingredients, pour over fish and marinate 1 hour in foil.

Place remaining fennel stalks in oven at 100°C (200°F) until dried out. Transfer dried fennel to the barbecue over hot coals. Barbecue fish over fennel for 5 minutes each side or until the fish flakes easily when tested. The fennel will burn, imparting an aromatic taste to the fish.

Serves 4

TALL HERBS
Plant tall-growing herbs at the back of your garden bed or tub. This makes harvesting easier.

Garlic bulbs and cloves (Allium sativum)

GARLIC

(ALLIUM SATIVUM)

Plant description: *Garlic is one of the most popular herbs in cooking and naturopathy. It likes a sunny spot with a sandy but rich soil, and grows well close to roses, being a deterrent to aphids. Plant single cloves in 5 cm deep drills in spring or autumn. Cover with soil and keep moist in dry weather. Strap leaves will emerge followed by a large pin-cushion flower. When both wither away, dig up the bulb (5–6 months after planting). Hang it in a cool, shady place where there is a good air circulation and when the bulbs harden they are ready.*

Uses: *Garlic has remarkable antiseptic and antibiotic properties. As a blood purifier, it can maintain a healthy body and is recommended as a regular part of your diet as a preventative medicine. It can also combat cold infections, expel worms, lower high blood pressure, act as a decongestant and cleanse the skin. Eat garlic in stews, with Italian dishes, eggs, lamb or vegetables. Rub the salad bowl with cut cloves or add them to mayonnaise and dressings. There are few places where garlic goes amiss.*

Garlic Chicken

Have no fear, you will not reek of garlic after eating this dish. Slow cooking in a sealed pot gives the chicken a golden hue with the most wonderful melt-in-the-mouth flavour. A leg of lamb may also be cooked in this same manner, though it will take an hour longer.

1.5 kg chicken
salt and freshly ground black pepper
3 tablespoons olive oil
1 bouquet garni
40 cloves garlic, peeled
1 cup white wine (250 mL)

PASTE
1 cup plain flour (125 g)
3 tablespoons water

Clean and dry chicken. Season inside and out with salt and pepper. Heat oil in a heavy flameproof casserole and brown chicken. Add bouquet garni, garlic and white wine. Cover with lid. To make paste, mix flour with water to a smooth consistency. Spread over the edge of the lid to seal pan. Bake in a 150°C (300°F) oven for 2 hours. Break pastry seal and serve chicken surrounded by a crown of garlic. Remove any fat from the juices and pour over chicken. Serve warm with crusty bread and a crisp salad.
Serves 4–6

Garlic Chicken

Herb and Garlic Stuffed Mushrooms

500 g firm mushroom caps
90 g butter
3 cloves garlic, crushed with a pinch salt
6 tablespoons chopped mixed herbs, such as parsley, chives dill, tarragon, chervil, marjoram, basil or thyme
2 tablespoons dry white wine
½ cup soft fresh breadcrumbs (30 g)
salt and freshly ground black pepper
extra butter, melted

Remove stalks from mushrooms, by twisting stems. Chop stalks finely. Melt butter in a heavy-based frying pan and saute chopped mushroom stalks for a few minutes. Add garlic, herbs and white wine. Sprinkle over the breadcrumbs and season with salt and freshly ground pepper. Use to fill the mushroom caps. Set the filled caps in a shallow greased dish. Brush with a little melted butter and bake in a 190°C (375°F) for 7 minutes or until golden brown. Serve at once.

Serves 6

Garlic Prawns

750 g green (uncooked) prawns
4 large cloves garlic
90 mL olive oil
2 bay leaves
⅓ cup aioli
1 sprig fresh thyme or ¼ teaspoon dried thyme
1 tablespoon lemon juice
freshly ground black pepper

Shell prawns leaving head and tail shell intact, then devein. Peel garlic and cut into slivers.

Heat oil in a heavy-based frying pan over moderate heat. Add garlic and cook until it starts to colour. Drain and discard.

Increase heat and when oil is moderately hot, 190°C (375°F), add prawns and bay leaves, stirring constantly until prawns are cooked (about 5 minutes).

Remove pan from heat and carefully stir through aioli, thyme and lemon juice to taste. Divide between individual serving plates and grind black pepper over each plate before serving. Serve hot with crusty bread.

Serves 4

Crunchy Vegetables with Garlic Dip

Serve this garlic 'salad' as an accompaniment to barbecued meats, or as a dip for fresh vegetables, such as cauliflower, celery or carrots.

1 bulb garlic, peeled
salt
8 thick slices stale white bread, crusts removed
juice 1–2 lemons
1 ½ cups olive oil (375 mL)

Puree garlic in a food processor with a good pinch salt. Soak bread briefly in cold water, squeeze well with your hands to remove excess water and add bread to garlic with half the lemon juice. Process until smooth. With motor still running, add oil in a slow, steady stream until a thick white paste has formed. Adjust seasonings, adding more lemon juice to taste if necessary.

Makes 3 cups (750 mL)

Crunchy Vegetables with Garlic Dip

GINGER

(Zingiber officinale)

Plant description: *Ginger is a perennial plant originating in Asia. It reaches about 1–1.5 m, and produces spikes of white and purple flowers. Requiring a warm to temperate climate, in colder climates it can be grown only under glass.*

Propagate from pieces of the rhizome (underground stem) which is the part used for cooking and is available from green-grocers. In early spring, place the pieces 2.5 cm below the surface of a rich, well-drained soil, add some lime or dolomite if you have acid soil, and cover with a good mulch on top. Keep soil damp but not wet. Ginger dislikes too much sun, so during a hot dry spell, cover with a shade cloth. Harvest the rhizomes in late summer, before they become too ropey.

Uses: *Ginger's powerful flavour is a must for curries, pickles and chutneys, and tastes delicious with steamed vegetables and Chinese dishes. It warms the stomach and stimulates the secretory juices, aiding purification of the body's system. It is often recommended as a therapeutic drink for colds.*

Delicious ginger root (Zingiber officinale)

Hot Mango and Tomato Chutney

4 medium firm under-ripe mangoes, peeled, seeded and diced
6 under-ripe tomatoes, sliced
1 cm piece ginger root, finely grated
2 cloves garlic, minced
2 onions, chopped
1 cup currants (150 g)
4 red chillies, seeded and sliced
2 tablespoons chopped fresh coriander
¼ teaspoon cayenne pepper
2 cups malt vinegar (500 mL)
2 cups brown sugar (350 g)
salt

Place all ingredients in a heavy-based saucepan. Mix well and bring to boil, then simmer gently for 10 minutes. Reduce heat to low and cook, stirring until mangoes are soft, and mixture is a jam-like consistency. Add salt to taste.

Remove from heat and cool slightly. Bottle chutney in sterilised jars. Remove any air bubbles by piercing mixture with a skewer. Cut out circles of greaseproof paper according to jar size. Place these on top of the chutney and press lightly with fingertips to remove air. Seal with sterilised lids. Store in a cool place and refrigerate after opening.

Makes 1.7 litres

Ingredients for Hot Mango and Tomato Chutney

Almond Fried Chicken with Spiced Ginger Sauce

2 kg chicken pieces
⅔ cup grated Parmesan cheese (80 g)
⅓ cup dry breadcrumbs (20 g)
¼ cup ground almonds (30 g)
salt and freshly ground black pepper, to taste
2 eggs
1 tablespoon milk
⅓ cup plain flour (40 g)
oil, for frying

SPICED GINGER SAUCE
1 tablespoon finely grated ginger root
1 teaspoon whole allspice
1 teaspoon whole peppercorns
½ teaspoon mustard seeds
½ teaspoon whole cloves
⅔ cup dry white wine (160 mL)
3 tablespoons white wine vinegar
2 tablespoons soy sauce

Remove skin from chicken pieces. Pat dry with paper towel. Combine Parmesan, breadcrumbs, almonds, salt and pepper. Set aside. In another bowl, blend together eggs and milk.

Dip chicken pieces in flour then egg-milk mixture then almond mixture. Heat oil in frying pan. Fry chicken portions gently for 10 minutes, turning to brown all sides. Drain on paper towel and serve hot or cold.

To make Spiced Ginger Sauce, combine ginger and spices in a mortar and pestle and crush lightly. If you do not have a mortar and pestle, place on a sheet of aluminium foil, fold the foil over and crush with a rolling pin. Combine white wine, vinegar and soy sauce in a small saucepan. Add spices and gently heat until boiling. Boil for 8 minutes then strain. Serve sauce in a shallow bowl suitable for dipping.
Serves 6

Gingered Green Beans

1 cm piece ginger root, finely grated
1 teaspoon ground fenugreek
500 g green beans, trimmed and diagonally sliced
2 tablespoons finely chopped fresh mint
1 teaspoon olive oil

Pour enough water into a saucepan to cover the bottom and heat. Add ginger and fenugreek and cook for 2 minutes. Add beans and mint and toss lightly. Cook over low heat until beans are just tender. Remove from saucepan and refrigerate until chilled. Toss in olive oil before serving.
Serves 6

HORSERADISH

(COCHLEARIA ARMORACIA)
Sometimes known as Cochlearia officinalis or Armoracia rusticana.

Plant description: *This perennial herb grows 80 cm tall and has large scalloped leaves and tiny white flowers. Its most valuable part is a hot-flavoured taproot. Horseradish likes semi-shade, plenty of water and above all, a well-dug soil to accommodate the taproot. Plant seedlings with their stems 2.5 cm below the soil. Lift the roots after one year's growth. Separate the taproot, clean and dry. Cut other roots into 10 cm lengths and replant at least 2.5 cm below the soil surface. The root is very persistent and the leaves are well loved by snails, so beware.*

Uses: *Horseradish has been used for centuries with shellfish, poultry, pork and beef. Medicinally, it purifies the blood and clears the sinuses, providing a good, all-round tonic and relief from colds. It also cures dogs' worms.*

Fresh Horseradish

There is nothing like fresh horseradish. The fresh roots will keep a long time in a cool dry place. To ensure a full fresh flavour, make horseradish in small batches and store in the refrigerator for up to three weeks.

6 tablespoons grated horseradish roots
2 teaspoons salt
2 tablespoons raw sugar
¼ cup vinegar (60 mL)

Wash roots and peel. Place in the container of a food processor and blend until finely chopped. Add salt, sugar and vinegar to taste.

Alternatively, grate into a small bowl and stir in salt, sugar and vinegar to taste. Pack into sterilised jars and refrigerate until required. Tastes delicious served with roast beef, oily fish and grilled steak.
Makes 200 mL

Horseradish (Cochlearia armoracia)

Broccoli Salad with Lime Mayonnaise

3 large heads broccoli, thick stems discarded
Italian Dressing

LIME MAYONNAISE
2 cups mayonnaise (500 mL)
2 cups light sour cream (500 mL)
⅓ cup lime juice (80 mL)
1 tablespoon finely grated lime peel
2 tablespoons grated horseradish root
1 tablespoon Dijon-style mustard

Pare bases of broccoli stems, place florets in a steamer and steam over boiling water until just tender (approximately 3 minutes). If you have only a small steamer this can be done in batches. When cooked, plunge instantly into iced water, taking care not to break the florets. Cool, cover with plastic wrap and refrigerate overnight.

When required to serve, sprinkle with Italian Dressing (see recipe) and serve with lime mayonnaise. To make lime mayonnaise, whisk ingredients together in a bowl. This dressing can be prepared in advance and stored in the refrigerator.
Serves 8–10

ITALIAN DRESSING
2 tablespoons Italian or French wine vinegar
½ clove garlic, crushed
salt and freshly ground black pepper
1 cup olive oil (250 mL)
1 tablespoon finely chopped parsley

Combine vinegar, garlic, salt and pepper. Gradually whisk in oil and garnish with parsley.
Makes 1½ cups (375 mL)

Barbecued Beef with Horseradish Cream Sauce

1.5 kg beef fillet or thick piece rump steak
4–6 rashers bacon

MARINADE
1 carrot, roughly chopped
1 onion, roughly chopped
1 cup port (250 mL)
½ cup oil (125 mL)
few peppercorns
1 teaspoon whole allspice
1 clove garlic, crushed

HORSERADISH CREAM SAUCE
1 cup thickened cream, whipped and chilled (250 mL)
1 tablespoon grated horseradish root
1 shallot, finely chopped
1 tablespoon finely chopped fresh parsley

Trim beef of excess fat and all sinew. Place on a board and wrap bacon around in a spiral fashion. Secure with toothpicks. Combine all marinade ingredients and place with beef in a shallow ceramic bowl. Cover with plastic wrap and marinate in the refrigerator overnight, turning beef from time to time. Remove beef from marinade and pat dry with paper towel.

Cook beef over moderately hot barbecue coals for about 10–12 minutes for a medium rare steak or 15–20 minutes for a medium steak. Test with a skewer then remove from barbecue and stand meat for 10 minutes before carving. Carve thin slices across the grain. Arrange on a platter and serve with Horseradish Cream Sauce.

To make sauce, combine all ingredients, stir until blended and serve in a bowl.
Serves 10

Horseradish Sour Cream Dressing

300 mL sour cream
3 tablespoons grated horseradish root
squeeze lemon juice
salt and freshly ground black pepper

Beat sour cream with horseradish and lemon juice. Season with salt and freshly ground pepper. Serve with beetroot and other salads.
Makes 1½ cups (375 mL)

Barbecued Beef with Horseradish Cream Sauce

Tomato Pasta and Ling with Horseradish and Sour Cream

salt
juice 1 large lemon
1 small carrot, 1 celery stalk and 1 parsley sprig, tied together
600 g ling fillets or other white-fleshed fish
500 g fresh tomato pasta, e.g. tagliatelle, spirelli
2 tablespoons grated horseradish root
1 tablespoon plain flour
400 mL sour cream
30g butter
1 teaspoon chopped fresh dill, plus few sprigs for decoration

In a large saucepan of cold water put some salt, the lemon juice and the vegetables and bring to the boil. Add ling and gently simmer until cooked through. Remove with a slotted spoon and set aside; discard vegetables. When ling has cooled slightly, cut into large serving pieces and keep warm. Bring the cooking water back to the boil, add pasta and cook until *al dente*.

In a small saucepan heat horseradish. Sprinkle flour over it and stir over a low heat until the flour browns slightly. Add sour cream and heat through; do not boil. Add butter and stir until it melts, then whisk in 1 tablespoon pasta cooking water and the chopped dill.

Drain the cooked pasta and transfer to a warm serving plate. Top with ling pieces, pour sauce over the top and add the sprigs of dill before serving immediately.

Serves 4

Tomato Pasta and Ling with Horseradish and Sour Cream

Lemon Grass (Cymbopogon citratus)

LEMON GRASS

(CYMBOPOGON CITRATUS)

Plant description: *This grass-like herb grows 60 cm–2 m high and quickly forms a thick clump, so leave plenty of room when planting. It appreciates copious watering, full sun and rich soil. To propagate, divide clumps and relocate.*

Uses: *Lemon Grass contains vitamin A and an aromatic oil frequently used in skin cosmetics. It is also a popular herb in Thai cookery. Chop fresh leaves into the teapot to make a healthy infusion for healthy eyes and skin.*

The fleshy white part at the base of the plant is also a popular ingredient in South-east Asian cooking. Sliced finely, or crushed to a paste with other herbs and spices, it gives a wonderful lemony taste to many dishes.

Squid and Prawn Hot Soup

250 g squid
1 litre chicken stock
1 stalk lemon grass or 2 strips lemon rind
50 g red king prawns
1–2 teaspoons fish sauce (see *Note*)
1–2 fresh chillies, seeded and sliced
2 garlic cloves, crushed
juice 1 lime
chopped fresh coriander, to garnish

Clean squid, cut body hood into strips and chop tentacles. Bring stock and lemon grass or rind to the boil, reduce heat and simmer for 5 minutes.

While stock is simmering, devein prawns and halve them. Add squid, prawns and half the fish sauce to the pan. Immediately stir through chillies. Taste and adjust seasoning.

Combine garlic and lime juice, stir through soup and serve hot, garnished with coriander.

Note: Thai fish sauce can be bought from most delicatessens and Asian groceries.

Serves 4–6

Lemon Grass and Chilli Prawns

These prawns are very spicy. To lessen the effect of the chilli, remove the seeds. Also, add only half the amount of masala suggested. The masala will keep for up to two weeks in the refrigerator if stored in a covered bowl.

1 kg green (uncooked) prawns
3 tablespoons oil, for frying

MASALA
1 onion, peeled
6 cloves garlic, peeled
½ teaspoon turmeric
1 cm piece cinnamon stick
1 cm piece ginger root, finely grated
20 fresh red chillies, (split and seeds removed if preferred)
grated rind and juice 1 lime or lemon
5 cm piece lemon grass, cut into 1 cm pieces

To make masala, place onion in the container of a food processor with garlic, turmeric, cinnamon stick, ginger and chillies. Blend until finely chopped. Add lime rind and juice. Stir through the lemon grass pieces.

Peel prawns, leaving tail intact and remove veins. Place in a glass or ceramic bowl and add half of the masala. Store remaining masala in a covered small bowl for another day. Stir to evenly distribute the mixture through the prawns. Cover and marinate for two hours in the refrigerator.

Heat oil in a wok or frying pan and add prawns. Stir-fry over high heat for 5 minutes or until just cooked. Serve hot with rice.

Serves 4

Squid and Prawn Hot Soup, and
Lemon Grass and Chilli Prawns

Lemon Grass Chicken

Shrimp paste (blanchan) gives this dish a wonderful flavour with the lemon grass. Before using the shrimp paste, wrap the amount required in a small piece of aluminium foil and roast in a dry frying pan for a few minutes. Cool and use as required.

1 onion
½ bunch shallots
4 stalks lemon grass, thinly sliced
1 teaspoon shrimp paste
1½ cups coconut milk (375 mL)
1 tablespoon raw sugar
pinch salt
1 tablespoon curry powder
juice 1 lemon
1 kg chicken pieces, skin removed
4 tablespoons oil
2 tablespoons sambal oelek (chilli paste)
½ cup water (125 mL)
2 lime leaves or ½ teaspoon lime peel
salt and freshly ground black pepper

Place onion, shallots, lemon grass, shrimp paste and ½ cup (125 mL) coconut milk in the container of a food processor. Blend to make a fine paste.

Mix sugar, salt and curry powder together in a small bowl. Rub chicken pieces with lemon juice. Spread curry mixture over chicken and leave to marinate for about one hour.

Heat oil in a heavy flameproof casserole. Add sambal oelek and cook for a minute, stirring. Add chicken and fry until golden brown. Add shallot-coconut mixture, the remaining coconut milk, water and lime leaves. Season and simmer uncovered for 35 minutes or until chicken is tender and sauce thickens slightly. Serve with steamed rice.
Serves 4–6

MARJORAM

(ORIGANUM MAJORANA)

Plant description: *Marjoram is a hardy, evergreen perennial suitable for pots or the open garden. It can be grown from seed and likes a sunny position, light soil and regular watering, though it can withstand drought quite well. It forms a compact bush, 25–75 cm tall depending on the variety, with little round leaves and white or purple flowers. Remove flowers for a stronger flavour in the leaves. Layer to take cuttings every few years, as plants deteriorate.*

Uses: *Marjoram is excellent with Italian dishes — tomato sauces, pasta and pizzas, and goes well with meat, pumpkin, potatoes and rice. It will strengthen and condition the hair and its oil, rubbed into aching joints and muscles, relieves stiffness. Marjoram has remarkable antiseptic qualities so a regular intake cleans the blood and keeps you free of tummy bugs. If you have a toothache, chew a few leaves.*

Marinaded Bocconcini

1½ cups olive oil (375 mL)
few sprigs fresh herbs such as rosemary, tarragon, dill, parsley, basil or marjoram
2 teaspoons cracked black pepper
6–8 small bocconcini or two small logs of chevre (See *Note*)

Heat oil with herbs and black pepper in a small pan until heat haze just rises; cool. Place the cheese into a wide-mouthed glass storage jar. If using chevre, cut into thick rounds and carefully place in jar.

Pour over cool oil and add a few fresh sprigs of herbs. Cover and store in the refrigerator for 2–5 days or until required. Serve sliced as a first course.
Note: Bocconcini and chevre are types of cheese.
Serves 4

Marjoram (Origanum majorana)

Herbed Green Beans

125 g butter
½ teaspoon chopped fresh marjoram
½ teaspoon chopped fresh basil
1 teaspoon chopped fresh parsley
1 teaspoon chopped chives
500 g green beans
1 small onion, chopped
1 clove garlic, chopped
freshly ground black pepper
3 tablespoons sunflower seeds, to serve
fresh chives, to garnish

Combine butter with marjoram, basil, parsley and chives and set aside. Place the beans in a saucepan with the onion and garlic and cover with boiling water. Cook until tender and drain. Add herb butter to the pan and swirl the beans around briefly until well coated. Season to taste and add sunflower seeds just before serving. Tie beans into bundles with chives before serving.
Serves 6

Pissaladiere

QUICK SCONE DOUGH
50 g butter
3 cups self-raising flour (375 g)
1 cup milk (250 mL), soured with 1
  teaspoon lemon juice

TOPPING
3 large onions, sliced
¼ cup oil (60 mL)
2 teaspoons chopped fresh marjoram
freshly ground black pepper

GARNISH
100 g anchovy fillets, drained
20 stuffed black olives

Preheat oven to 220°C (425°F). Rub butter into flour and mix in milk to make a firm dough. Turn dough onto floured board and knead lightly. Pat out to round shape 23 cm in diameter. Place on greased baking sheet. Using forefinger and thumb, raise edge slightly by pinching the dough.

To make topping, fry onions in oil, until soft but not browned. Stir in marjoram. Spread onions over top of dough. Arrange anchovy fillets in a lattice over the onions, placing an olive in each square formed.

Bake for 20–25 minutes, until base is browned.

Serves 3–4

Pissaladiere and Marinaded Bocconcini

MINT

APPLEMINT (MENTHA ROTUNDIFOLIA or M. SUAVEOLENS)
PEPPERMINT (M. PIPERITA)
SPEARMINT (M. SPICATA)

Plant description: *There are many different types of mint, and all are easy to grow. With a tendency to put down roots all over the garden, they are best grown in containers. All like their roots cool, so water regularly. Peppermint, eau-de-cologne mint and spearmint prefer semi-shade, while other varieties can withstand full sun.*

Keep the different types away from one another, as they will cross-fertilise, adulterating one another's flavours. Prune well to prevent them becoming straggly and to encourage new growth.

Peppermint (Mentha piperita)

Uses: *All the mint flavours are slightly different but all go well with lamb, young vegetables, fruit and cool drinks. Applemint and peppermint are the best mints for cooking.*

Applemint, with its round, woolly leaves and pale mauve flower spikes, exudes a powerful apple fragrance and flavour. It likes a light soil and of all the mints, is the most resistant to mint rust.

The pinky mauve flowers, small purplish leaves and reddish stems of peppermint emit a pepperminty scent when touched. Peppermint oil contains menthol, useful in the treatment of sprains, bruises, toothache and blocked sinuses. Peppermint tea aids indigestion, flatulence, improves the appetite and is a general good tonic.

Spearmint also makes a refreshing tea and aids digestion, dispelling flatulence.

Minty Potato Salad

Chunky warm potato salad flavoured with fresh mint has always been a favourite, especially during summer. Pick the mint fresh from the garden, just before using.

1 kg old potatoes
salt
2 onions, chopped
6 tablespoons chopped fresh mint
¾ cup mayonnaise (180 mL)

Peel and halve potatoes. Cook in boiling salted water until just tender to the point of a knife; drain. Cut hot potatoes roughly and carefully slide into a bowl. Sprinkle over chopped onions and fold mint leaves through the potatoes with mayonnaise. Serve warm or at room temperature.

VARIATION:
Peel and roughly chop 3 hard-boiled eggs. Fold through the potatoes.
Serves 4–6

WHICH MINT?
With over 40 varieties of mint to choose from, enthusiastic cooks may well wonder which mint to choose. Generally, mint recipes use applemint (*Mentha rotundifolia*) or peppermint (*M. piperita*), but part of the joy of herbs is discovering new flavours and taste combinations, so experiment until you find the mint you prefer.

Fresh Fruits with Mint

¼ small sugar melon
½ pineapple
3 peaches
3 nectarines
4 kiwi fruit
1 punnet strawberries (250 g)
2 bananas
juice 1 lemon
2 tablespoons caster sugar
6 tablespoons chopped fresh mint

Remove seeds from sugar melon and cut into chunks. Cut pineapple into pieces. Peel peaches and nectarines and remove stones. Cut fruit into quarters or eighths. Peel kiwi fruit and slice. Wash and hull strawberries, halve if large. Place all the fruit in a large serving bowl. Peel and slice bananas over just before serving. Pour over lemon juice and sprinkle over caster sugar. Scatter over snipped mint. Refrigerate until ready to serve.
Serves 6

Fresh Fruits with Mint can use any combination of seasonal fresh fruit

Racks of Lamb with Parsley Mint Crust

60 g butter
1 tablespoon mango chutney
2 teaspoons French mustard
1 clove garlic, crushed
2 teaspoons lemon juice
6 racks lamb (4 chops each), excess fat trimmed
6 tablespoons finely chopped fresh parsley
2 tablespoons finely chopped fresh mint
salt and freshly ground black pepper
2 mangoes, peeled, seeded and sliced

MANGO MINT SAUCE
1 mango, peeled, seeded and pureed
1 tablespoon finely chopped fresh mint
freshly ground black pepper
1 teaspoon vinegar

Combine butter, chutney, mustard, garlic and lemon juice. Spread evenly over the back of each lamb chop. Sprinkle over parsley and mint, and press onto lamb using the back of a metal spoon. Season well with salt and pepper and cook in an oven preheated to 200°C (400°F) for 20–30 minutes or until tender.

To make sauce, combine ingredients in a small saucepan. Heat gently then serve.

Serves 6

Tomato Granita

8 tomatoes, peeled and finely chopped
2 shallots, finely chopped
1 stalk celery, finely chopped
1 clove garlic, crushed
1 cucumber
1 teaspoon chopped fresh mint
mint leaves, for decoration

Strain tomatoes to remove excess liquid and seeds. Mix shallots, celery and garlic with tomatoes and pour into ice cream trays. Freeze until solid.

Ten minutes before serving, remove from the freezer to soften a little. Peel cucumber and chop into very fine dice. Break up tomato ice with a fork and stir in cucumber and mint. Serve in individual glass dishes. Garnish with mint leaves.

Serves 4

Mint Sauce

Serve with roast lamb.

1 bunch fresh mint leaves
2 tablespoons raw sugar
3 tablespoons malt vinegar
¼ cup boiling water (60 mL)

Chop mint leaves finely and place in a small bowl with sugar and vinegar. Pour over the boiling water. Cool and serve at room temperature.

Makes about 1 cup (250 mL)

Above: Spearmint (Mentha spicata)
Below: Racks of Lamb with Parsley Mint Crust

OREGANO

(ORIGANUM VULGARE)

Plant description: *Also known as wild marjoram, this plant is in fact the original parent plant of the sweet marjoram we use so often in the garden today. Its flavour and uses are similar, too. It grows to 75 cm and is an ideal container plant. Easy to grow from seed, it will propagate itself by layering. It likes a light soil, sunny and sheltered position and regular watering.*

Uses: *Use sparingly as it has a powerful flavour. Goes well with tomatoes and onions, pasta and grilled steak.*

Oregano (Oreganum vulgare)

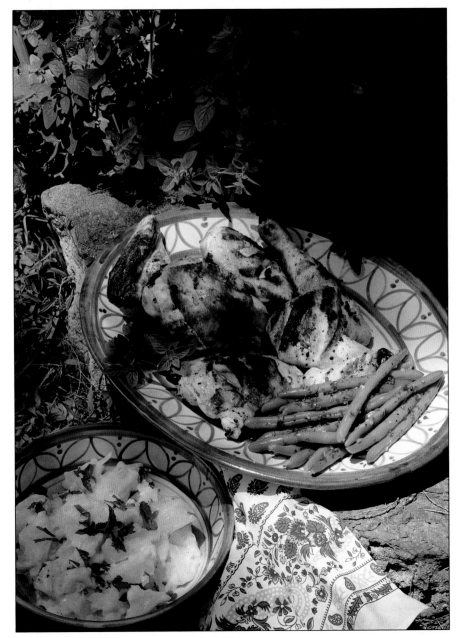

Barbecued Chicken with Oregano

The first time I came across this dish was in a small restaurant in the Algarve in southern Portugal. We could smell this delicious aroma of barbecuing chicken and the pungent perfume of the oregano wafting down from a rooftop restaurant. The flavour lived up to expectations. Serve with a simple salad and a rice pilaf.

1 kg chicken pieces
2 teaspoons salt
grated rind and juice 2 lemons
½ cup olive oil (125 mL)
freshly ground black pepper
4 tablespoons fresh oregano, roughly
 chopped

Place chicken in a glass or ceramic dish. Rub pieces well with salt. Whisk lemon juice, rind, oil, pepper and oregano together in a small bowl. Pour marinade over chicken, turning the pieces to coat thoroughly. Cover with plastic wrap and marinate in the refrigerator overnight.
 Barbeque the chicken pieces over medium to high heat; 12 minutes for breast meat or wings, 15–20 minutes for thighs and legs, turning frequently to prevent burning. Brush with the marinade during cooking.
 Serves 4

Barbecued Chicken with Oregano, served with Herbed Green Beans and Minty Potato Salad

PARSLEY

(Petroselinum crispum)

Plant description: *There are several varieties of parsley, the best known being curly-leaved parsley and flat-leaved (Italian) parsley. Biennials usually treated as annuals, they like a sunny position, and a rich, well-dug, moist soil. Both are suitable for containers and the curly-leaved variety makes a decorative border for flowerbeds. Height varies between 15–60 cm.*

Parsley is a slow germinating seed. To speed it up a bit, soak the seeds prior to planting. Use a nitrogenous, rich, light seed compost, keep it constantly moist and be patient: it can take up to eight weeks to appear.

Uses: *All varieties are excellent for good health — they are particularly good sources of vitamin A, C and iron. They also contain vitamin B, sodium, calcium, and magnesium. This herb keeps the digestive system in good working order and especially the kidneys. Making parsley part of your regular diet will undoubtedly benefit your health.*

Chop parsley leaves into practically any dish — salads, soup, vegetables or fish. Use dried parsley in winter. Munch a little raw parsley to sweeten the breath or drink parsley tea to remove excess body fluid — just the thing for slimmers.

Parsley (Petroselinum crispum)

Herb Pasta with Garlic Cream Sauce

250 g fresh Herb Pasta (see recipe)

GARLIC CREAM SAUCE
2 tablespoons olive oil
3 cloves garlic, crushed with a pinch salt
3 tablespoons chopped mixed fresh herbs, basil, marjoram, chives, chervil, coriander or thyme
3 tablespoons chopped fresh parsley
¾ cup cream (180 mL)
salt and freshly ground black pepper

Cook pasta in a large pan of boiling salted water until *al dente.*

To make sauce, heat oil in a large heavy-based frying pan and fry garlic until golden. Stir through herbs and cream. Season and bring to the boil. Simmer for 2 minutes.

Drain pasta well. Return to the rinsed out saucepan and add sauce. Serve at once.

Serves 4

Ossobuco alla Milanese

Italians, like most Europeans, consider bone marrow a great delicacy, and either suck it out or scoop it out with a special spoon.

ossobuco or shin of veal cut into 8 cm x 5 cm slices
plain flour
80 g butter
1 very small onion, thinly sliced
1 small carrot, sliced
1 small piece celery, sliced
1 clove garlic, sliced
salt and freshly ground black pepper
1 glass white wine (100 mL)
500 g canned peeled tomatoes
1 cup broth (can be made with stock cubes) 250 mL

GREMOLATA
4 tablespoons chopped fresh parsley
1 clove garlic, finely chopped
grated peel 1 lemon or orange

Flour ossobuco and brown slices in butter. Add onion, carrot, celery and garlic to the pan. Season and stir occasionally, turning veal to seal it. When everything in the pan has acquired a lovely golden colour, add wine and let it evaporate almost completely.

Add sieved tomatoes and cook slowly for just over an hour or until the meat is so tender, it falls easily from the bone. If sauce becomes too thick, add a few tablespoons of broth. Before serving, lift out ossobuco and arrange on a heated serving dish.

Make gremolata by adding chopped parsley, garlic and lemon peel to the sauce in the pan, stir it through and pouring it over the ossobuco.

Serves 4

Tabbouli

Tabbouli is readily available from most delicatessens or sandwich shops these days, but homemade has a far better flavour. Once you've tried this recipe, you'll use no other. Chop the shallot, parsley and mint in a blender or food processor with the steel blade fitted to make this easy salad even easier.

¾ cup burghul (cracked wheat) 140 g
2 tomatoes
½ bunch shallots, finely chopped
1½ bunches Italian parsley, finely chopped
6 tablespoons finely chopped mint
juice 1 large lemon
3–4 tablespoons olive oil
salt and freshly ground black pepper

Soak burghul in water to cover for 5 minutes. Drain in a sieve and squeeze out as much water as possible with your hands. Roughly chop tomatoes. Place burghul in a salad bowl with shallots, parsley and mint. Pour over lemon juice and oil. Season well with salt and freshly ground pepper and lightly fork through the chopped tomato.

Serves 4–6

Omelette aux Fines Herbes

5 fresh eggs
¼ cup cream (60 mL)
2 tablespoons water
salt and freshly ground black pepper
30 g unsalted butter
4 tablespoons finely chopped fresh parsley, chervil, chives and tarragon

Break eggs into a bowl. Add cream and water, and season to taste. Beat lightly with a fork until frothy.

Melt butter in a 20 cm omelette pan until foaming. Pour in egg mixture, tilting pan to coat evenly. Cook until the underside is golden and the uppermost still soft. Sprinkle over the herbs and lightly fork through. Fold the omelette in half and slide out onto a warmed plate. Cut in half and serve at once.
Serves 2

Parsley and Walnut Soup

The flavour combination is delicious in this light soup. Use sweet fresh walnuts, or the canned Californian variety.

200 g sweet fresh walnuts
60 g butter
2 leeks, sliced and washed
1½ bunches Italian parsley leaves
2 cups chicken stock, or water and stock cubes (500 mL)
salt and freshly ground black pepper
4 tablespoons creme fraiche

Blanch walnuts in boiling salted water for 3 minutes and refresh under cold water. Rub the nuts in a tea towel, then between your fingers to remove skins.

Melt butter in a heavy saucepan. Add leeks and parsley, cover closely with a piece of greaseproof paper and cover with a lid. Sweat over a low heat for 5 minutes. Remove paper and add walnuts and chicken stock. Bring to the boil and simmer for 10 minutes.

Blend soup until smooth in a food processor. Season and return to saucepan. Reheat and stir through creme fraiche.
Serves 4

Parsley and Walnut Soup and Omelette aux Fines Herbes

Rosemary (Rosmarinus officinalis)

Rosemary Lamb Cooked on a Bed of Potatoes

This is one of my favourite ways of serving a leg of lamb. The vegetable bed collects all the lovely juices from the lamb as well as flavouring the leg and keeping it moist. It is important though to use a very lean leg of lamb or remove most of the fat. Serve cut thickly accompanied by the vegetables and a seasonal green vegetable, lightly steamed.

1.5 kg lean leg lamb
2 cloves garlic
3 tablespoons fresh rosemary sprigs
salt and freshly ground black pepper
2 tablespoons olive oil
3 leeks, sliced and washed
1 kg old potatoes
1½ cups beef stock (375 mL)

Remove any surplus fat from leg of lamb. Peel garlic and cut into slivers. Season surface of lamb with salt and pepper. With a sharp knife, make small incisions under the skin of the lamb. Insert a sliver of garlic and a small sprig of rosemary into each.

Heat oil in a heavy-based baking dish and fry leeks until soft and translucent. Peel potatoes and slice thinly. Add to the leeks in the pan, layering the leeks through potatoes. Mix through remaining sprigs of rosemary. Pour over well-seasoned stock. Place lamb on vegetable bed and bake in a 190°C (375°F) oven for 20 minutes. Lower heat to 150°C (300°F) and bake for a further 40 minutes for pink lamb, 1 hour for a medium cooked lamb. Serve sliced thickly with the vegetables.

Serves 4-6

ROSEMARY

(ROSMARINUS OFFICINALIS)

Plant description: *Rosemary is a slow-growing herb from the Mediterranean that can live for 30 years. Able to withstand hot sun and drought conditions, it is ideal for a rockery, particularly the prostrate variety. With tough, silvery leaves and sometimes blue, sometimes white, flowers you can make it a pretty border plant, or clip it to form a hedge in any shape you like. It will also live happily in a pot. Liking a sandy soil, it is particularly suitable for seaside gardens. To propagate, strike cuttings with a woody heel.*

Uses: *You can use this evergreen all year round. Especially good with lamb, rosemary also tastes delicious with veal, pork, poultry and vegetables, but use sparingly. Rosemary water revitalises the scalp and tones the skin. Its oil makes a wonderful hair conditioner and can be rubbed into forehead and temples to relieve a tension headache. Dried leaves add fragrance to potpourri, sachets and moth bags.*

Rosemary Lamb Cooked on a Bed of Potatoes

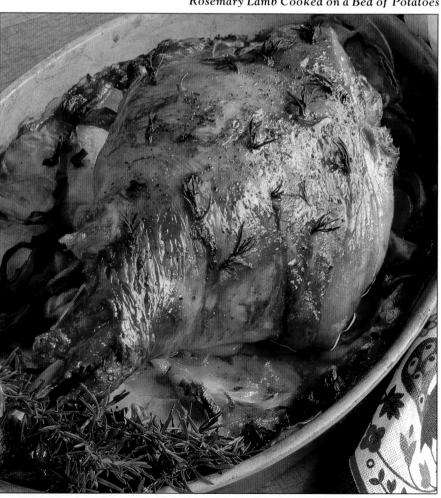

SAGE

(SALVIA OFFICINALIS)

Plant description: *Purple and broad-leaved varieties of sage are also commonly available but garden sage has the better flavour. It is a hardy, perennial shrub that grows 60 cm high on poor but alkaline soil, so add lime or dolomite if necessary or if growing in a pot, make sure it's made of concrete. It dislikes overwatering and wet weather and is prone to caterpillars but the greyish green, rough-textured leaves and purple flowers make a handsome plant. Pinch out growing tips or cut back to keep it compact. Seeds are slow to germinate but propagation is easy by layering.*

Uses: *Besides its well-known use in sage and onion stuffing, sage gives many meat dishes a special flavour and just a few leaves chopped into salads, soups or cold drinks can be delicious.*

The Chinese have valued sage tea for centuries as a therapeutic tonic believed to ease rheumatism, stimulate the brain and its senses, aid the memory and sooth the nerves. It also strengthens gums and darkens greying hair. Use fresh sage whenever possible: dried sage is not so tasty.

Sage (Salvia officinalis)

Sage and Onion Sausage Rolls

1 tablespoon olive oil
1 onion, finely chopped
500 g good quality sausage mince
3 tablespoons chopped fresh sage or
** 2 teaspoons dried sage**
2 tablespoons chopped fresh parsley
salt and freshly ground black pepper
250 g shortcrust pastry
1 egg, beaten with a pinch salt

Heat oil in a heavy-based frying pan and cook onion until softened. Place sausage mince in a bowl and add onion, sage and parsley. Season with salt and pepper.

Cut prepared pastry in halves. Roll each piece out thinly to a rectangle 36 cm x 12 cm. Trim edges to neaten. Pile sausage mixture down the centre of each strip. Brush edges with beaten egg and bring pastry over the meat, overlapping slightly. Cut across into 6 cm lengths and place seam side down on a baking tray. Brush with beaten egg and make a few slits in each for steam vents. Bake in a 190°C oven (375°F) for 15 minutes or until golden brown and cooked. Serve warm.

Makes 1 dozen

Sage and Cheese Damper

This damper is excellent served straight from the oven. I often make it the morning of a picnic and pack it warm, wrapped in a towelling cloth, to be eaten out-of-doors. Or if you are feeling really adventurous, cook it in a bush oven. Make the dough and cut into two. Cover both rounds with the onion and cheese topping and wrap each in a double thickness of aluminium foil, leaving room for the damper to rise. Bury the foil parcels in the glowing ashes of the bush fire. Cook for 20 minutes, turning once.

TOPPING
2 onions, chopped
3 tablespoons olive oil
1½ tablespoons chopped fresh sage
2 cloves garlic, crushed
30 g butter

DAMPER
4 cups self-raising flour (500 g)
1 teaspoon salt
60 g butter
1 tablespoon chopped fresh sage or ½
** teaspoon dried sage**
1½ cups grated Cheddar cheese
** (185 g)**
1½ cups soured milk and water
** (375 mL) mixed with juice of ½**
** lemon**

Cook onions gently in oil until soft and tender. Stir through sage. Melt butter and saute garlic lightly. Set aside.

Sift flour and salt into a large mixing bowl. Rub in butter until mixture resembles fine breadcrumbs. Stir through the chopped sage and ¾ cup of the grated cheese (90 g). Make a well in the centre and stir in soured milk, water and lemon juice mixture using a knife. Gather mixture into a soft dough. Turn out onto a lightly floured surface and gather roughly into a round. Do not knead.

Place the round on a lightly greased baking tray and press out to about 4–5 cm thick. Score the surface into eighths and brush with garlic butter. Cover with onion and sage topping and sprinkle over remaining cheese. Bake in a preheated oven 200°C (400°F) for 35 minutes or until well risen and a good crusty golden brown.

Serve hot.

Honey Duckling with Sage, Potato and Onion Stuffing, served with fresh sage, roast turnips and freshly cooked asparagus

Honey Duckling with Sage, Potato and Onion Stuffing

2 kg duckling
1 cup water (250 mL)
¼ cup honey (90 g)

STUFFING
2 large old potatoes, peeled
30 g butter
3 large onions, chopped
1½ tablespoons chopped fresh sage
**   leaves or 1½ teaspoons dried sage**
salt and freshly ground black pepper

To make stuffing, cook potatoes in boiling salted water until tender. Drain and mash. Melt butter in a large frying pan and cook onions until very soft, without colouring. Combine onions, potatoes and sage. Season with salt and freshly ground pepper.

   Wipe duck with kitchen paper. Insert stuffing, truss with string and set on a rack in a roasting pan. Pour in water and roast duck for 15 minutes in a 200°C (400°F) oven. Reduce heat to 160°C (325°F) and roast for a further 1 hour. Brush duck with warmed honey 10 minutes before the end of cooking time.

   To serve, cut duck into quarters. Serve with the stuffing, and vegetables of your choice.

   Serves 4

Sorrel

(Rumex acetosa)

Plant description: *Sorrel is a hardy perennial that grows best in semi-shade, 45–90 cm tall. Small greenish or reddish flowers appear in summer. It is easy to grow from seed and to propagate by root division in the autumn.*

Uses: *Cook the big flat leaves as a tasty vegetable on their own — it tastes a bit like lemony spinach — or chop the leaves sparingly into a salad. Sorrel is tasty in soups and sauces. Make sorrel puree each summer and freeze it for use all year round.*

The slightly bitter flavour you can taste is oxalic acid, which gives sorrel its wonderful blood cleansing qualities. Add a few leaves in the blender when making your healthy vegetable juice and you will be keeping your liver and kidneys in good working order. However, use sparingly — too much oxalic acid can cause poisoning and kidney problems. The leaves are also effective as a poultice for boils or other skin eruptions.

Sorrel (Rumex acetosa)

Sorrel and Potato Soup

2 large potatoes
60 g butter
salt and freshly ground black pepper
2 bunches fresh sorrel
2 cups chicken stock (500 mL)
¾ cup water (180 mL)
¾ cup cream (180 mL)
few chives, for garnish

Peel and thinly slice potatoes. Melt butter in heavy-based saucepan. Add potatoes and season well with salt and pepper.

Cover closely with a piece of greaseproof paper. Cover with the lid and cook over very low heat for about 7 minutes.

Rinse sorrel and add to the pan. Cover closely and cook for a further 2 minutes. Remove paper and pour over chicken stock and water. Bring to the boil and simmer for 20 minutes.

Pour soup into the container of a food processor in small lots and blend until smooth. Return to pan and stir through cream. Reheat without boiling. Serve hot with snipped chives scattered over.

Serves 4

Salmon Cutlets and Sorrel Cream Sauce, served with steamed vegetables

Salmon Cutlets and Sorrel Cream Sauce

4–6 salmon cutlets (150–200 g each)
freshly ground black pepper
60 g unsalted butter

SORREL CREAM SAUCE
60 g unsalted butter
2 French shallots, chopped
1 cup creme fraiche (250 mL)
juice ½ lemon
8 sorrel leaves
salt and freshly ground black pepper

Season salmon cutlets with pepper. Heat butter in a heavy-based frying pan.

Quickly cook salmon until golden, about 3–4 minutes on each side. This will vary depending on the thickness of the cutlets. Test by gently prying the flesh apart. If it pulls away easily, the cutlet is cooked. Be careful not to overcook the salmon.

To make the sauce, melt butter and cook shallots gently until softened. Add creme fraiche and lemon juice. Bring to the boil and simmer gently for 1 minute. Remove stems from sorrel and slice leaves into strips. Add to pan and cook for 2 minutes; season.

Place salmon cutlets on a heated serving dish and spoon over the warm sauce. Serve immediately.

Serves 4

TARRAGON

FRENCH TARRAGON (ARTEMISIA DRACUNCULUS)
RUSSIAN TARRAGON (A. DRACUNCULOIDES)

Plant description: *Of the two varieties of tarragon, French is reputed to have the better flavour, while Russian is considered the more robust. Tarragon needs full sun to prosper, growing to 1 m with tiny white or yellow flowers and narrow green leaves. It may vanish in winter but its creeping roots ensure that next spring it will pop up again. To keep stock healthy, divide the roots with a spade in spring every three or four years and start new plants. Dry tarragon stems at the end of the growing season to tide you over the winter months.*

Uses: *Tarragon is almost entirely a culinary herb. It has a sharp but sweet taste which gives tarragon vinegar, mustard and sauce a very distinctive flavour. It also goes well with poultry, fish and vegetables but should never be cooked for a long time as it becomes bitter.*

Poached Tarragon Chicken

1.5 kg chicken
juice 1 lemon
60 g butter
salt and freshly ground black pepper
1 onion, peeled and quartered
bay leaf
few sprigs fresh parsley
½ stalk celery
1 large carrot, peeled and quartered
few sprigs fresh tarragon or
 1 tablespoon dried tarragon (reserve a few sprigs for garnish)
2 egg yolks
1 cup creme fraiche (250 mL)

Wipe chicken inside and out with kitchen paper. Rub over with lemon juice. Melt butter in a heavy flameproof casserole and brown chicken, all sides until golden. Season with salt and pepper, add onion, bay leaf, parsley, celery, carrot and tarragon. Cover with cold water and bring to the boil. Place lid over and simmer slowly for 1 hour.

Remove chicken and cut into serving size pieces. Keep warm while making sauce. Reduce cooking liquid to 1 cup (250 mL). Beat egg yolks in a small bowl. Strain over cooking liquid, whisking with a balloon whisk. Return liquid to saucepan and whisk until sauce is thickened. Add creme fraiche and stir to heat through. Spoon over chicken and garnish with fresh tarragon.

Serves 4

Tarragon Mushrooms a la Grecque

500 g button mushrooms
2 tablespoons chopped fresh tarragon or 1 tablespoon dried tarragon
juice 1 lemon
2 cloves garlic, crushed with a pinch salt
3 tablespoons chopped fresh parsley
1 ripe tomato
salt and freshly ground black pepper
1 bay leaf
¼ cup olive oil (60 mL)
1 cup water (250 mL)

Wipe mushrooms and trim stalks. Place in heavy-based saucepan with tarragon, lemon juice, garlic and parsley. Peel and remove seeds from tomato, roughly chop. Add to the pan with remaining ingredients. Bring to the boil, cover and simmer gently for 8 minutes. Serve hot or chilled, with crusty bread or as an accompaniment to barbecued meats.

Serves 4 as a side dish

DRYING
Use the microwave for drying herbs. A teacup full of fresh tarragon leaves, for instance, can be crushed to powder after two or three minutes in the microwave.

Left: French tarragon (Artemisia dracunculus)
Below: Tarragon Mushrooms a la Grecque, and Thyme and Pecan Chicken Galantine served with cherry tomatoes, fresh thyme and sprouts

THYME

GARDEN THYME (THYMUS VULGARIS)
LEMON THYME (T. CITRIODORUS)
CARAWAY THYME (T. HERBA BARONA)

Plant description: *There are over 40 varieties of thyme. All are evergreen perennials, varying in height 5–45 cm with very pretty, tiny mauve flowers. They like a sunny position, well-drained soil and are quite at home in a rockery, between pavers or a container — the heat from nearby bricks or stones increases their pungent aroma. Don't use artificial fertilisers on thyme as they make the leaves drop and go yellow. Most varieties tend to spread and can be propagated by root division. They are also easy to grow from seed.*

Garden thyme is the most common, producing the best oil and the best pollen from bees that visit its small flowers.

Uses: *Traditionally thyme is associated with flavouring meat, but zucchini, carrots and tomatoes benefit from its flavour, too. Thyme is also an essential ingredient in bouquet garni.*

They all have medicinal as well as culinary uses since they contain high concentrations of thymol, a powerful antiseptic. Thyme oil, applied to the forehead and temples, soothes an aching head while thyme tea makes a refreshing antiseptic drink, clearing infections in the throat during a cold. It also aids digestion and bowel disorders.

Watercress Soup, and Watercress and Smoked Salmon Log

Lemon thyme (Thymus citriodorus) above, and garden thyme (Thymus vulgaris) below

Roast Turkey with Lemon Thyme and Parsley Stuffing

Our Christmas wouldn't be the same if we didn't use this stuffing!

6–8 kg turkey

STUFFING
185 g butter
2 onions, chopped
4 cups fresh wholegrain breadcrumbs (240 g)
2 tablespoons fresh lemon thyme leaves
6 tablespoons chopped fresh parsley
grated rind 2 lemons
2 eggs, beaten
salt and freshly ground black pepper

Melt butter in a frying pan and add the chopped onions. Saute for 5 minutes or until translucent. Place breadcrumbs in a large bowl with lemon thyme and parsley. Add onions, butter and lemon rind. Mix through using a fork. Add eggs to breadcrumbs. Season well. Use to stuff the cavity of a turkey or chicken.
    Serves 6

Thyme and Pecan Chicken Galantine

2.5–3 kg chicken, boned

STUFFING
60 g butter
2 onions, peeled and chopped
500 g pork and veal mince
¾ cup pecans (75 g)
¼ cup chopped dried apricots (35 g)
⅔ cup fresh breadcrumbs (40 g)
1 egg, beaten
salt and freshly ground black pepper
2 teaspoons fresh thyme leaves
extra fresh thyme, to garnish

Melt butter in a heavy-based frying pan and cook onions until softened. Combine in a bowl with mince, pecans, apricots, breadcrumbs and beaten egg. Season well with salt, pepper and thyme.

    Stuff boned chicken, tucking in the wings and legs to form a neat roll. Tie with string, securing ends first with metal skewers. Place in a baking pan and roast in a 180°C (350°F) oven for 1½ hours, covering with foil if it browns too quickly. Leave to cool, and refrigerate overnight. Remove strings and slice thinly. Serve with a crisp salad.
    Serves 4–6

WATERCRESS

(NASTURTIUM OFFICINALE)

Plant description: *A perennial plant growing to 45 cm, watercress has dark green, fleshy leaves with small white flowers during late spring and summer. It grows well in semi-shade near water. It is high in vitamin C, iron and iodine.*

Uses: *Watercress leaves make delicious sandwiches, salads, soup and garnish. Use only in small quantities. Pregnant women and those with kidney problems should avoid using it at all.*

Medicinally, watercress has been recommended for gout, tuberculosis, catarrh, anaemia, eczema and mild digestive disturbances.

Watercress (Nasturtium officinale)

Watercress Soup

The pungent peppery flavour of the watercress comes through beautifully in this soup. May be served hot or chilled.

½ **bunch watercress**
60 g butter
2 onions, chopped
1 large potato, peeled and diced
salt and freshly ground black pepper
2½ cups chicken stock (625 mL)
2 tablespoons plain flour
⅔ **cup cream (160 mL)**

Wash watercress and reserve a cupful of young sprigs for garnish. Chop remainder, stalks and all. Melt half the butter in a heavy-based saucepan and add onions, potato and chopped watercress. Season well and cover with a piece of grease-proof paper. Cover with lid and sweat over a low heat for 10 minutes. Remove paper, add chicken stock to pan, bring to the boil and simmer for 15 minutes. Blend in a food processor or blender until smooth, strain into a bowl.

Melt remaining butter in rinsed-out saucepan. Stir in flour. Add soup gradually, stirring. Bring to the boil, stir in cream and adjust seasonings. Just before serving garnish with reserved watercress sprigs. Serve hot or cold.

Serves 4

Watercress and Smoked Salmon Logs

1 long French breadstick
¾ cup mayonnaise (180 mL)
300 g smoked salmon slices
1 Spanish onion, thinly sliced
freshly ground black pepper
2 cups watercress sprigs
2–3 tablespoons vinaigrette
3 tablespoons fresh dill sprigs

Split the French breadstick lengthways. Remove some of the bread centre. Spread halves thickly with mayonnaise. Lay smoked salmon over each half, top with onion and season with pepper. Toss watercress sprigs in vinaigrette. Cover both halves then sprinkle with dill.

Press halves together and wrap securely with foil. Chill until required. To serve, separate the halves and cut into 10 cm lengths.
Serves 4

Watercress Hollandaise

1 bunch watercress leaves
3 egg yolks
pinch salt
freshly ground black pepper
juice ½ lemon
185 g unsalted butter

Blanch watercress in boiling salted water. Drain and rinse under cold water. Squeeze out as much water as possible.

Place egg yolks, salt, pepper and half the lemon juice in a food processor and blend for half a minute. Melt butter until foaming. With motor running, add sizzling butter in a slow steady stream. Add watercress and blend until smooth. Taste sauce, adding remainder of the lemon juice to taste. Transfer to a bowl and serve warm.

The sauce may be reheated or kept warm by placing the bowl in a small pan of simmering water.
Makes 1 cup (250 mL)

QUANTITIES OF HERBS
All the recipes in this book suggest how much of any herb to use e.g. 3 tablespoons or ½ bunch. However, as everyone responds to the flavour of herbs differently, use your discretion and test as you cook.

Poached Oysters with Watercress Sauce

24 oysters, in the shell
1–2 lemons
1 bunch watercress
1 bouquet garni
1 tablespoon finely chopped onion
1 tablespoon finely chopped carrot
cream, to mix
½ cup dry white wine (125 mL)
1 cup water (250 mL)

Remove oysters from shell and place in a bowl with their liquid. Carefully peel rind of lemons, making sure no pith is included. Cut lemon rind into julienne strips (matchsticks) and blanch in boiling water for 3 minutes. Drain, refresh in cold running water and set aside.

Pick leaves from watercress. Wash well then blanch in boiling water for 4 minutes. Drain well and puree in a blender or food processor. Measure ⅔ cup of puree (160 mL) and dilute with cream so it will coat an oyster. Keep warm.

Place remaining ingredients in a pan and simmer for 5 minutes. Remove vegetables and bouquet garni. Add oysters to pan and poach over a gentle heat for 2 minutes. Drain and put oysters back in shells.

Divide oysters between four serving plates and coat with sauce. Garnish with lemon strips.
Serves 4

To serve Poached Oysters with Watercress Sauce, drain oysters after heating through, and replace them in shells

---

WHICH HERB FOR WHAT FOOD

Angelica	used crystallised in cakes, biscuits, marmalades
Anise	fresh leaves used in salads, steamed vegetables, shellfish; aniseed used in cookies, apple pie
Basil	pesto, tomato dishes, eggs, mushrooms, green salads, pasta
Bay	part of bouquet garni, used in stews, soups, poached fish, marinades; single leaf sometimes used in milk puddings
Bergamot	young leaves good in salads and with pork
Caraway	seeds flavour breads, cakes, biscuits, pasta, cabbage, parsnips, turnips, peas, baked apples
Chervil	part of *fines herbes* traditionally used with eggs, chicken, fish, salads, soups and sauces; chervil soup is also delicious
Chives	omelettes, salads, soups, mayonnaise, cream cheese
Coriander	seeds indispensable to curries, pickled fruit; whole fresh leaves used with fish, cauliflower, beetroot, celery
Dill	leaves and seeds go well with soups, salads, white sauces, egg dishes, seafood, cheese, pickles and vinegar
Fennel	fresh leaves or seeds taste good in soups, fish, cottage cheese, bread, cakes
Garlic	stews, Italian dishes, omelettes, lamb, vegetables

curly-leaved parsley
basil
sage
flat-leaved parsley
coriander
bush basil
rosemary
lemon thyme
thyme
variegated thyme
dill
garlic chives
marjoram
chives
oregano
mint
tarragon

Ginger	curries, pickles, chutneys, vegetables, Chinese cooking, cakes and biscuits
Horseradish	shellfish, poultry, pork, beef
Hyssop	rabbit, lamb, salads, vegetables, drinks, stewed peaches, apricots
Lemon balm	summer drinks, salads, pork, lamb, chicken stuffings
Lemon verbena	fruit salads, punches, summer drinks
Lemon grass	Thai cooking, curries, salads
Lovage	soups, stews, salads, sauces
Marjoram	Italian dishes, tomatoes, pumpkin, potatoes, meat, chicken and rice
Mint	lamb, young vegetables, fruit salad and cool summer drinks
Nasturtium	salads, sandwiches, cream cheese
Oregano	see Marjoram
Parsley	part of bouquet garni used in stews and meat dishes; fresh leaves go with almost anything — salads, fish, soups, vegetables, stews
Sage	stuffings, meat, salads, soups, cold drinks
Salad burnet	salads, fruit, fruity cups and summer drinks
Savory	sauces, drinks, vegetables e.g. peas, beans, squash
Sorrel	salads, soups, sauces, vegetable purees
Tarragon	chicken, fish, vegetables
Thyme	essential for bouquet garni used in casseroles and meat dishes; also goes well with zucchinis, tomatoes

Watercress Salad

1 bunch watercress
½ punnet mustard cress
½ bunch fresh spearmint, chopped
½ bunch chives, snipped
1 small Spanish onion, sliced
1 ripe avocado

DRESSING
1 tablespoon mayonnaise
2 tablespoons herb vinegar
1 teaspoon green peppercorns
2 tablespoons chopped fresh parsley
4 tablespoons hazelnut or good olive oil
salt and freshly ground black pepper

Wash watercress and pick over the bunch. Use young tips only, reserve stalks for soup. Arrange watercress in a bowl with mustard cress, spearmint, chives and Spanish onion. Peel and slice avocado and add to salad.

To make dressing, place mayonnaise, vinegar, peppercorns, parsley and oil in a small bowl and whisk together. Season with salt and pepper. Pour over salad just before serving. Lightly toss.

Serves 4

FRAGRANT FLAVOURS

Candied and crystallised flowers, petals and leaves, have been used for centuries as sweet meats. Exquisitely decorative, they preserve the plant by coating it in sugar which crystallises with repeated boiling and evaporation.

Lorna Rose

*Honeysuckle (*Lonicera *species)*

Victoria Sandwich

Delicious as a simple sponge or decorated as a birthday cake, this is a very useful basic recipe.

125 g butter
½ cup caster sugar (110 g)
2 eggs
1 cup self-raising flour (125 g)
3 tablespoons jam
icing sugar
1 cup cream, whipped (250 mL)

Preheat oven to 175°C (340°F). Cream butter and sugar until soft. Whisk eggs, beat into sugar mixture. Fold in flour. Spoon mixture into two greased and lined 15 cm sponge tins. Bake for 20 minutes. Remove cakes from tins and cool on cake rack.

Spread jam onto first cake and sandwich to second with one-third of the whipped cream. Spread top of cake with remaining whipped cream and decorate with crystallised flowers and petals.

SERVING SUGGESTIONS:
Try decorating your cake with some of the following: crystallised petals and leaves, candied blossoms, fresh flowers, small toys, marzipan miniature fruits, smarties, jaffas or other sweets, hundreds and thousands, glace fruits, silver balls, whipped cream, sliced fresh fruit, candles and anything else that appeals to your imagination.

CANDIED AND CRYSTALLISED
What is the difference between candied and crystallised fruits and flowers? Very little. Candied fruits are preserved by boiling with sugar until a thick syrup forms. Crystallised fruits are also boiled with sugar and then rolled in extra sugar to coat with crystals. Blossoms or petals are too delicate to be boiled, so the sugar syrup is poured over them and they are left to set.

Candied Blossoms

Sweet flowers such as roses, violets, wattle, honeysuckle, sweet peas and scented geraniums, are all edible. They are exquisite when candied and used to decorate a special dessert or cake, and can add that crowning glory to a homemade ice cream or sorbet. Alternatively, you can offer them in a bowl as a sweet.

3 cups or handfuls edible blooms
(weight depends on choice of flower)
2 cups water (500 mL)
3 cups granulated sugar (750 g)

Wash the flowers briefly but very carefully. Remove stems and gently pat dry. Place water and sugar in a heavy-based saucepan and heat slowly to dissolve sugar. Once sugar has dissolved, bring to the boil and boil until small cracks form, 138°C (270°F). Pour about half the syrup into a shallow pan. Let both quantities cool. Position the flowers on a metal rack inside the pan so that they float on the syrup. Cover with a cloth and leave to stand in a cool place for several hours. Spoon over the remaining syrup to completely cover the flowers. Cover again with a cloth and stand for at least 12 hours in a cool place.

Remove the rack and place it on a tray to drain. Leave until the flowers are completely dry. Store flowers in an airtight container with sheets of baking paper between each flower to prevent them from sticking to each other.

Crystallised Petals and Leaves

Sugar-coated herb petals and leaves are a beautiful way to preserve herbs. Use to decorate desserts or cakes, or offer as a sweet with coffee.

1 cup edible petals or herb leaves
(weight depends on flower chosen)
1 egg white
tiny pinch salt
fine vanilla-spiced or caster sugar

Wash petals or leaves carefully. Pat dry gently with absorbent kitchen paper (do not rinse wattle). Leave flowers whole if very small. Beat egg white with the salt until foamy. Brush it on each petal, flower or leaf with a pastry brush or your fingers. Surfaces should be moist but with no excess egg white.

Shake or dust sugar on both sides. Place gently on a tray lined with baking paper. Dry in the refrigerator for 2–3 days. Store in an airtight container in the refrigerator until required.

Below: Candying sweet peas
Right: Cakes can be beautifully decorated with candied and crystallised flowers

Rose Geranium Sorbet

This is a favourite dessert, ideal to serve with curries when entertaining. Growing rose geraniums just outside your kitchen on a sunny deck or patio is easy and extremely useful. Added to a refreshing lemon sorbet, a few leaves turn the sorbet a beautiful pale green and have the most wonderful perfume and flavour.

Rose Geranium Sorbet

185 g sugar
2½ cups water (625 mL)
6 lemons
4 (6 if small) rose geranium leaves, crumpled
1 egg white
extra leaves, for decoration

Place sugar in a medium-sized saucepan with water. Grate over lemon rind. Heat over low heat and when sugar has dissolved, bring to the boil. Add crushed leaves. Boil for 6 minutes; cool.

Squeeze juice from the lemons and strain into cooled syrup. Pour mixture into cold freezer trays or a metal bowl. Place in a freezer until mixture just begins to freeze. Remove, turn into a bowl and discard geranium leaves. Beat with a whisk until smooth, but not melted. Beat egg white until stiff but not dry, fold lightly through mixture and return to tray. Cover and freeze until firm.

Pile sorbet into chilled glasses and serve decorated with a rose geranium flower and leaves.

Serves 2–4

Rose geranium (Pelargonium graveolens)

Heartsease (Viola species)

Heart-shaped Biscuits

1 cup plain flour (125 g)
60 g butter
½ cup sifted icing sugar (90 g)
2 egg yolks
vanilla icing sugar, to dust

Sift flour onto a work surface and make a well in the centre. Place butter in the centre and sift over icing sugar. Rub butter and sugar between the fingertips of one hand until creamy. Add egg yolks and vanilla. Sweep around with your other hand, gathering the flour into the centre. Mix to form a soft dough. Knead very lightly, wrap in a piece of plastic wrap and chill for 10 minutes.

Roll dough out on a lightly floured surface until very thin. Using a 5.5 cm heart-shaped cutter, cut out hearts and set on a baking tray. Bake in a 190°C (375°F) oven for 12 minutes or until biscuits are a pale golden colour. Cool on a wire rack. Dust with icing sugar and store in an airtight tin until required.

Makes 24

GERANIUMS
Rose geranium (_Pelargonium graveolens_)
Peppermint geranium (_P. tomentosum_)
Coconut geranium (_P. enossularoides_)
Lemon geranium (_P. limonium_)

Plant description: Geraniums can be planted anywhere, including rockeries. They need sun and can withstand dryness and great heat. Hardy perennials, all have highly perfumed leaves with small, undistinctive flowers that repel most garden pests. They are all quick land colonisers and fast growers.

Rose geranium has a bushy upright habit and a delicious smell. Peppermint geranium is low-growing and trailing. Lemon geranium grows into a 2 m tall bush and emits a very strong perfume. Coconut geranium smells, as its name suggests, of coconut and is the only scented geranium suitable for inclusion in a potpourri.

Uses: Bruised lemon or rose geraniums add fragrance to finger bowls, and a leaf or two in milk puddings, jellies and egg custards adds a piquant flavour. Try placing a crushed handful of scented geranium leaves under the hot tap, for a fragrant bath.

Sweet Violets and Wild Strawberries

1 bunch sweet violets
1 punnet strawberries or alpine strawberries (250 g)
1 punnet blueberries (250 g)
1 tablespoon caster sugar
1 tablespoon lemon juice

CINNAMON CREAM
1 cup creme fraiche
1 teaspoon cinnamon
1 tablespoon caster sugar
grated rind 1 orange
1 tablespoon orange juice

Remove stems from violets. Rinse strawberries and blueberries. Place in a bowl and fold through caster sugar and lemon juice.

To make Cinnamon Cream, beat creme fraiche with cinnamon, caster sugar and orange rind. Fold through juice and spoon into a bowl. Chill until required. Serve with Heart-shaped Biscuits (see recipe).

SCENTED SUGAR
Vanilla sugar is well known and available commercially. It is also easily made by storing a vanilla bean in a jar with caster sugar. Well, what about using scented geranium leaves for a change?

Scented geraniums are among the most fragrant plants in the herb garden. The variety available includes almond, apple, lemon, lime, nutmeg, peppermint and rose geranium. The flavour of these leaves is easily transferred to sugar, by simply layering a handful through a jar of caster sugar. Rose petals, violets, wattle and mints will do the same. Leave the leaves, flowers or petals in the container of sugar and close tightly for a couple of weeks. Use to flavour cakes, biscuits, custards, creams, sorbets, ice cream or even tea.

Violet (Viola odorata)

BREAD AND BUTTER

Herb breads have been enjoyed for centuries. For those who like baking their own bread, simply add a pinch of your favourite dried herbs to a basic bread recipe.

Herb Bread

1 small French breadstick
125 g favourite herb butter

Cut bread into diagonal slices, keeping the loaf intact by leaving the base of each slice attached.

Make the herb butter according to the directions given in the recipe, keeping the butter softened. Spread thickly on both sides of each slice of bread. Wrap loaf in a large sheet of foil. Place in a preheated 200°C (400°F) oven for 10 minutes or until the butter has melted. Open the foil parcel a few minutes before the end of cooking time to crispen the loaf if liked.

Serve hot.

Herb breads and a selection of herb butters

Herb Butters

Herb butters are an invaluable part of cooking, used to flavour a variety of dishes. Maitre d'hotel, a famous butter made with butter, lemon juice and parsley, is used for grilled fish, grilled chicken and pan-fried veal escalopes. Rosemary Butter goes beautifully with loin of lamb or can be used to add flavour to steamed vegetables accompanying a lamb or veal dish. And of course herb butters in any shape or form are ideal to flavour a French breadstick to make herb bread. Herb butters may be frozen for up to three months if well wrapped in a double layer of freezer wrap or aluminium foil.

Garlic, or Anchovy and Herb Butters are delicious with barbecued meat, but you can use them with whatever you like. A chilled dish of herbed butter makes a wonderful addition to a simple meal.

Chive Butter

125 g butter
2 teaspoons lemon juice
½ bunch chives, snipped
1 teaspoon grated lemon rind

Cream butter until softened. Beat in lemon juice. Fold through chives and lemon rind. Spoon butter onto a piece of plastic wrap, freezer wrap or aluminium foil. Form into a log shape and chill until firm. Cut off and use as required. Fresh herb butters may be frozen for up to three months.
Makes ½ cup (125 g)

Rosemary Butter

125 g butter
2 teaspoons rosemary spears
freshly ground black pepper
2 teaspoons lemon juice
1 teaspoon Dijon-style mustard

Cream butter in a bowl and fold through rosemary. Season with black pepper, lemon juice and mustard. Spoon onto a sheet of plastic wrap, freezer film or aluminium foil. Form into a log shape and chill or freeze until required.
Makes ½ cup (125 g)

Garlic and Herb Butter

250 g butter
4–5 cloves garlic, crushed with a large pinch salt
3 tablespoons chopped, mixed fresh herbs such as parsley, chives, marjoram, oregano or rosemary
2 tablespoons chopped shallots

Cream butter in a bowl until softened. Stir through crushed garlic, mixed herbs and shallots. Spoon butter onto a piece of plastic wrap, freezer wrap or aluminium foil. Form into a log shape and chill until firm. Cut off and use as required. Alternatively, place butter in a small pot and use while cooking barbecued meats. Use to butter a French breakstick for herb and garlic bread.

Makes 1 cup (250 g)

Anchovy and Herb Butter

250 g butter
5 anchovy fillets
6 tablespoons finely chopped mixed herbs, such as parsley, chives, basil, chervil or marjoram
freshly ground black pepper
grated rind and juice ½ lemon

Cream butter in a bowl until softened. Drain oil from anchovy fillets and mash until smooth, using the back of a fork. Fold through butter with herbs, black pepper, lemon rind and juice. Spoon onto a piece of plastic wrap, freezer film or aluminium foil. Form into a log shape and chill or freeze until required. Use to flavour barbecued steak both during cooking and as an accompaniment.

Makes 1 cup (250 g)

Tarragon Butter

A very delicately flavoured butter. Use with chicken while roasting or spread a dob of butter on steamed vegetables.

125 g unsalted butter
1½ tablespoons chopped fresh tarragon or 1½ teaspoons dried
2 teaspoons lemon juice

Cream butter until softened in a bowl. Stir through tarragon and lemon juice. Spoon onto a piece of plastic wrap, freezer wrap or aluminium foil and form into a log shape. Chill until ready to use.

Makes ½ cup (125 g)

Stuffed Nasturtium Leaves

Herbed Cream Cheese

Serve with crusty French bread or melba toast.

1 cup creamed cottage cheese or farm cheese (250g)
1 clove garlic, crushed with a pinch salt
freshly ground black pepper
juice ½ lemon
6 tablespoons chopped fresh herbs, such as parsley, basil, oregano
¼ bunch chives, snipped

In a bowl combine cottage cheese, garlic, pepper, lemon juice and herbs. Spoon into a serving bowl and chill until ready to serve. Serve with crusty French bread, melba toast or crudites.

Makes about 1½ cups (375 g)

NASTURTIUM — VITAMIN C, NATURALLY
Nasturtium (*Tropaeolum majus*)

Plant description: hardy annual to 30 cm. In an open, sunny position it will flower from summer to winter.

Uses: High in vitamin C, iron and sulphur, colourful nasturtium flowers and their pretty round leaves have a pleasantly peppery flavour. Add spice to your salad or cream cheese sandwiches, while improving your health.

*Nasturtiums (*Tropaeolum majus*)*

Stuffed Nasturtium Leaves

This is an ideal salad if you have nasturtiums growing in your garden. Pick the leaves and wash well — remembering to check for snails. The flowers can be used as a garnish for this unusual recipe. Nasturtium buds can be pickled and taste very similar to capers.

24–30 nasturtium leaves, very well washed
1 quantity Herbed Cream Cheese (see recipe)
paprika, to taste
nasturtium flowers, to garnish

Shake the leaves dry. Spread a thick layer of herb cheese over one half of each leaf. Fold the other half of the leaf over and press lightly to seal. Do not completely close. Lightly sprinkle exposed cheese with paprika. Chill and serve garnished with nasturtium flowers.

Serves 6–8, depending on the size of the leaves

KITCHEN ESSENTIALS

Herbs are essential in the kitchen. They are a basic ingredient in stocks and classic sauces and they add flavour to vinegars and oils to liven up salads. See the chapter on Gracious Gifts for details on the traditional bouquet garni and fines herbes.

Necessary equipment can be as simple as a chopping board and a small sharp knife. Some recipes call for you to lightly 'bruise' fresh herbs. This is most easily done in a mortar and pestle, preferably made of marble or earthenware. Bruising herbs with the pestle releases their flavours quickly.

Many herbs are suitable for making vinegars

Pesto Mayonnaise

Serve as a dressing over pasta salad or as an accompaniment to cold meats. Vary the consistency by adding a little water to the finished dressing, depending on how you are going to use the mayonnaise.

3 egg yolks
1 tablespoon Dijon-style mustard
1 tablespoon white wine vinegar
3 cloves garlic, peeled
1½ cups olive oil (375 mL)
salt and freshly ground black pepper
9 tablespoons fresh basil leaves
3 tablespoons parsley leaves
3 tablespoons grated Parmesan

Place egg yolks in a food processor with a metal blade fitted. Add mustard, vinegar and garlic and process until smooth. With motor running, add oil in a slow steady stream until a thick mayonnaise has formed. Season to taste. Add basil and parsley leaves, blend until smooth. Add Parmesan and blend until combined. The mayonnaise should be of a coating consistency; if it is too thick, add a little water.
   Makes 2 cups (500 mL)

Left: Useful equipment: a mortar and pestle (wooden or ceramic), a china mixing bowl, a copper pan and a mezzaluna ('half moon' in Italian) with a wooden bowl to avoid blunting the large metal blade
Below: Pesto Mayonnaise

Mayonnaise

3 egg yolks
1 tablespoon Dijon-style mustard
pinch salt
freshly ground black pepper
2 tablespoons lemon juice
1½–2 cups good olive oil (375–500 mL)

Place egg yolks, mustard, salt, pepper and lemon juice in the container of a food processor or blender and blend for 30 seconds. With motor running, dribble in oil in a slow steady stream until all oil is incorporated. Taste and correct seasonings if necessary.
   Makes 2 cups (500 mL)

Aioli

This delicious garlic mayonnaise goes particularly well with fresh seafood.

12–16 cloves garlic, coarsely chopped
3 egg yolks
salt and freshly ground black pepper
2 cups good olive oil (500 mL)
juice 2 lemons

Puree garlic and egg yolks in a food processor or blender. Add salt and pepper. With motor still running, add oil in a thin stream, slowly at first. As the sauce thickens, add lemon juice and taste, adding a little more lemon juice, salt or pepper if necessary.
   Makes 2½ cups (625 mL)

Tzatziki Dressing

1 medium-sized green cucumber
2 cloves garlic, crushed with salt
1½ cups unflavoured yoghurt (375 mL)
freshly ground black pepper
1 tablespoon chopped fresh mint

Peel cucumber, halve and scoop out seeds. Grate cucumber finely into a bowl. Drain away some of the cucumber liquid. Add garlic and yoghurt. Beat with a wooden spoon until pureed. Season with black pepper and stir through chopped mint.
   Makes 2 cups (500 mL)

Sauce Bearnaise

Sauce Bearnaise

Bearnaise sauce goes well with grilled steaks, fish or chicken. It is a beautifully rich sauce, so serve it sparingly.

⅓ cup white wine vinegar (80 mL)
2 shallots, chopped
1 bay leaf
few peppercorns
1 tablespoon dried tarragon
3 egg yolks
pinch salt
185 g unsalted butter
1 extra teaspoon chopped fresh tarragon

Place vinegar, shallots, bay leaf, peppercorns and tarragon in a small saucepan. Bring to the boil. Simmer to reduce liquid to 1 tablespoon. Strain and cool.
   Place egg yolks in the container of a food processor with a metal blade fitted and add reduced cooled vinegar with the salt. Melt butter until foaming. With the motor running, add sizzling butter in a slow steady stream. Add tarragon and taste for seasoning. Serve warm.
   Note: If sauce is to be reheated or kept warm, set the bowl in a small pan of hot water, stirring frequently.
   Makes about 1 cup (250 mL)

OIL AND VINEGAR — ESSENTIAL FOR SUCCESS

VINEGAR

Vinegar is the liquid product of an acid fermentation process of various grains and fruits. For instance, white wine vinegar is the acidic product of white wine, likewise cider vinegar of apple juice and malt vinegar of malt liquor.

Vinegars vary greatly in strength and flavour, according to their base. Vinegar is an essential ingredient in salads. The fresh acid cleans the palate and brings out the full flavour of salad vegetables.

Lemon juice, yoghurt, buttermilk and soy sauce also provide this element when used in a salad, however vinegar is the main ingredient used.

The most popular vinegars for use in salad dressings are: champagne vinegar, cider vinegar, red wine vinegar, rice vinegar and white wine vinegar.

Fruit vinegar: Combine 1 litre wine vinegar with 2 cups soft fruits such as raspberries, strawberries, blueberries, pears, peaches or plums (weight will vary according to fruit). Stir to lightly bruise the fruit. Cover and leave to infuse for two days. Bring to just boiling point. Strain the vinegar through a double piece of cheesecloth into clean sterilised bottles. Cork and label.

Herb infused vinegar: Combine 1 litre wine vinegar with 6 tablespoons bruised fresh herbs in a glass or earthenware bowl. Cover and leave to infuse for two weeks. Strain through a double piece of cheesecloth into clean sterilised bottles. Add a sprig of the fresh herb to each bottle. Cork and label.

OIL

The foundation of a good dressing is the oil and vinegar. The carefully balanced combination of these is important to bring out the full flavour of the salad. The kind of oil used depends greatly on the type of salad.

Almond oil, hazelnut oil and walnut oil: These are a delight to use in a dressing. They have a good nutty flavour that complements many a salad.

Chilli oil: Warm 2 cups olive oil (500 mL) and pour into a clean bottle with 1–2 tablespoons chopped Birds-eye chillies. Cap and store in a cool, dark place. Ready to use after two weeks.

Corn oil, peanut oil, safflower oil and sunflower oil: All polyunsaturated oils. They are light with little flavour and may be used in combination with one of the other more full-bodied oils to lighten a particular dressing. Used alone they tend to lack flavour.

Grapeseed oil: Has a good nutty flavour and is light.

Herb infused oil: Warm 2 cups olive oil (500 mL) and pour into a clean jar with 3 tablespoons fresh herbs. Cover and leave to steep for two weeks. Strain the oil through a fine cheesecloth into a bottle and store in a cool, dark place until required.

Olive oil: Possibly the most widely used oil, not only in salads but also in cooking. Its range of flavours and smoothness makes it the supreme oil. The oil is produced from pressing ripe to not-so-ripe olives. Grades vary with each pressing. Extra virgin oil is the best as it is the first oil released from the pressing. It is clear, often green, with a good, strong olive flavour. Use olive oil when you want that distinctive olive flavour. It's worth experimenting with olive oils to find one that suits your tastes and requirements.

Sesame oil: Has a strong sesame flavour. Use sparingly as it can sometimes overpower the salad.

Herb Vinegar

1 litre wine vinegar
6 tablespoons fresh herbs
extra sprig fresh herb

Combine vinegar with fresh herbs, bruised slightly in a glass or earthenware bowl. Cover and leave to infuse for two weeks. Strain through a double piece of cheesecloth into clean, sterilised bottles. Add a sprig of fresh herb to each bottle, cork and label.
Makes 1 litre

Herb Infused Oil

2 cups olive oil (500 mL)
3 tablespoons fresh herbs
extra sprig fresh herb

Warm olive oil and pour into a clean jar with fresh herbs. Cover and leave to steep for two weeks. Strain oil through a fine cheesecloth into a bottle. Add a sprig of fresh herb to each bottle, seal and label. Store in a cool dark place until required.
Makes 2 cups (500 mL)

Herb Vinaigrette

TO MAKE ⅓ CUP (80 mL):
1 tablespoon Dijon-style mustard
1 tablespoon white wine vinegar
1 tablespoon chopped fresh herbs,
such as chives, parsley, marjoram,
thyme, mint
4 tablespoons olive oil
salt and freshly ground black pepper

TO MAKE 1 CUP (250 mL):
2 tablespoons Dijon-style mustard
3 tablespoons white wine vinegar
3 tablespoons chopped fresh herbs,
such as chives, parsley, marjoram,
thyme or mint
¾ cup olive oil (180 mL)
salt and freshly ground black pepper

Place mustard in a bowl and whisk in vinegar and herbs. Gradually whisk in oil until mixture thickens. Season with salt and freshly ground pepper.

This dressing may be made and stored in the refrigerator until required. Add fresh herbs just before serving if liked.

A split clove or two of garlic may also be added.

Note: Varying the type of oil or vinegar, or adding lemon juice, will give you a different dressing every time. Also, the flavour will change dramatically every time you vary the herbs.

Oil and Vinegar Dressing

¼ cup white wine vinegar (60 mL)
pinch salt
pinch dry mustard powder
½ cup salad oil (125 mL)
freshly ground black pepper
2 tablespoons chopped fresh parsley
or a combination of parsley and
tarragon

Beat vinegar in a bowl with salt and mustard powder. Gradually add oil, drop by drop, and season with pepper. Stir in optional herbs and pour dressing over the salad of your choice just before serving.
Makes ¾ cup (180 mL)

Left to right: red wine vinegar, herb infused vinegar, corn oil, virgin olive oil, walnut oil, sesame oil, grapeseed oil

HERBS FOR ALL SEASONS

In the best of all possible worlds, you would use fresh herbs all year round, but many herbs are annuals and even perennials often die back in winter, so we have to make do with dried ones. If a recipe stipulates a quantity of fresh herbs, you can always replace it with one-third to one-quarter the amount of dried.

Although dried herbs lose some natural oils and vitamins, they still retain much of their flavour if correctly dried, and they are indispensible when the garden is bare. Dried herbs do eventually lose their flavour and become stale, however, so if you have jars of dried herbs over a year old, throw them out and start again. Store all your herbs in small, glass, airtight containers and never position the herb rack near a heat source, such as the stove, as the herbs will lose their flavour even faster.

HARVESTING

Wait until the new leaves or flower buds are beginning to unfurl. Pick your herbs immediately after the morning sun has evaporated the dew but before the heat of the day has begun. Herbs are at their most potent then. Never harvest herbs in wet or humid conditions.

The time of year for harvesting, as a general rule, is any time when the leaves, flowers, seeds or roots (depending on which part you are wanting) are well advanced but still young and fresh. Seeds must be collected from the old flower heads when they are mature (often they are brown and brittle).

All species of lavender can be harvested and dried easily

DRYING

Dry herbs on racks, slats or simply hang them upside down by their stems in a dry, cool place with good air circulation. You can use flyscreen frames or make your own by stretching muslin or hessian over an old picture frame. The important thing is that the air should reach every part of the plant. Lay the herbs out so they have plenty of space and turn them every few days. Never put them in the sun as this robs them of their colour, fragrance and valuable properties.

If you are gathering them into bunches, keep these small and as loose as possible, so that herbs in the middle of the bunch dry as well as those on the outside. When the leaves or flowers are so dry they become crackly, strip them from their stalks and store them. Label the jar with its name and date.

Hang bundles of herbs upside down to dry

A good short cut is to use your microwave oven. Lay out fresh herbs on absorbent paper, place in the oven, and cool on LOW for 3 minutes.

To collect seeds from herbs, such as dill, fennel and caraway, cut stalks carrying flower heads, place them in a paper bag head-first and secure with a rubber band tied around the top. Rub the stalk heads by hand through the paper bag.

For herbs which are valued for their roots, such as horseradish, valerian and dandelion, dig up the roots and wash them thoroughly, removing any hairs or unappetising parts. Cut roots lengthways into 1 cm wide strips and lay them out, on your herb drying racks or in the oven, on a very low heat with the door slightly ajar. Keep a close eye on them in the oven or they may burn. To test for dryness, try snapping the lengths in half — if they bend but refuse to break, they need more drying. When dry, store the roots in tissue paper in an airtight, labelled jar. Grate the roots as required.

FREEZING

Some herbs, like parsley and chives, are better frozen than dried. Pick only the strong young leaves. Wash and chop them, then wrap them in aluminium foil and label. Make up parcels small enough for a single meal, so you don't need to open them more than once. These should keep for two months. For longer-term storage, blanch before freezing.

A selection of fresh and dried herbs

GRACIOUS GIFTS

Herbs are the most adaptable plants in the world and for this reason they form the basis of many gifts. A present from your own garden, prepared by your own hands, is a very personal thing and the recipient will cherish it all the more, knowing the care you have taken with it.

Giving a person herbs is always an opportunity to be artistic in your packaging and labelling. Choosing the right container can be as much a part of the gift as picking the herbs at the right time of day. That's not to say that your gift need not be useful. Herbs are practical, too. Homemade bouquets garnis and *fines herbes* make excellent gifts. Here are a few ideas for the kind of gifts you can so easily make from the herb garden.

POTPOURRI

This is a wonderful way of keeping all the rooms in your house smelling fresh and fragrant. If you like, you can make each room smell different. There is nothing so sweet as catching a drift of perfume from bowls of potpourri. Place them on tables beside sofas or beds for the most noticeable aroma.

Potpourri is a fragrant mixture of flower petals, herbs, ground spices, seeds and barks, preserved with a fixative that both blends the different fragrances and slows down the release of the flowers' natural

Potpourri can look very beautiful

oils. To enhance the aroma, you can add a little concentrated oil or essence, available from chemists, to the mixture but don't get too carried away.

There are two ways of making potpourri. The more traditional method is a wet preparation, using only partially-dried flower petals, while the more decorative and popular method today is dry preparation.

Suitable flower petals for the basis of a potpourri are: roses, lavender, philadelphus (mock orange), violets, lily of the valley, red bergamot and white jasmine. Suitable fragrant herbs are sage, bay, lemon balm, eau-de-cologne mint, peppermint, bergamot, rosemary and lemon verbena. Spice favourites include cinnamon sticks, ground cloves and ground coriander seeds. You can put in flowers and buds other than those with a scent, if they dry well, to add colour and bulk to the collection: use marigolds, pansies, cornflowers, hyssop, borage, wattle, bougainvillea and nasturtiums. Dried orange and lemon peel can also add a refreshing aroma to potpourri. Cut only the best peel, avoiding any pith. Dry on paper in a warm oven and store in a dry, dark place until ready for use.

Three fixatives are suitable for potpourri — gum of benzoin, orris root powder and salt. The first two of these are available from chemists.

WET POTPOURRI

Place a layer of partially-dried flowers in the bottom of an earthenware crock. Sprinkle a layer of ordinary salt on top. Add another layer of flowers and another layer of salt. Continue in this way to the top of the pot. Cover and leave in a cool, airy place for a couple of weeks. Mix in the fragrant dried herbs with a wooden spoon. Seal and leave for another six weeks. Then add a few drops of oil or essence and leave, sealed, for a further two weeks. The preparation is then ready to be spooned into containers.

DRY POTPOURRI

Collect the flower petals in the early morning, after the dew has dried but before the full sun has robbed them of their essential oils.

Lay each petal or flower head out separately on paper in a cool, airy place and leave to dry. Don't allow the flowers to touch one another or they will stick together. Only when they are completely dried, are they ready for the potpourri.

To collect enough fragrant flowers, you will have to build up quite a collection. Pick and dry a few each fine day and store in an airtight container until you have enough to make a potpourri.

Rose Potpourri

3 cups rose petals
1 cup lavender or violet flowers
1 cup rose geranium leaves
1 cup mixed dried flower heads and buds
½ cup rosemary leaves
2 sticks cinnamon, coarsely-ground
20–30 coarsely ground cloves
1 cup fixative
4 drops rose essence

Mix all dry ingredients together. Add drops of essence and mix again. Store the mixture in an airtight container for six weeks. Tip out into small bowls and decorate with colourful dried petals or flowers.

Australian Bush Potpourri

4 cups *Eucalpytus citriodora* or *E. nicholii* leaves, or 2 cups of each, mixed
1 cup boronia flowers and foliage
2 cups wattle flowers
a selection of gum nuts
1 cup dried kangaroo paw flowers, for colour
1 cup fixative
5 drops eucalyptus oil

Prepare as for rose potpourri.

A great variety of herbs and flowers can be included in your potpourri

POMANDERS

The word 'pomander' comes from *pomme d'ambre*, which means apple of ambergris. Originally, the perfume of a pomander (which was worn around the neck or waist) was derived from ambergris, which comes from the intestines of the sperm whale. These days ambergris is not very popular and pomanders are made from lemons or oranges, studded with cloves and rolled in powdered orris root and cinnamon powder. They are associated with Christmas and make excellent gifts. Make your pomanders at least a month before Christmas. Choose freshly picked thin-skinned oranges or lemons and if you cannot push the cloves in, then use a meat skewer or toothpick to make the holes through the skin first. Put in as many cloves as you can fit. When the fruits are well covered with powdered orris root and cinnamon, put each pomander in a separate paper bag and leave it in a dark place for a month. When ready, remove and decorate it with ribbons, lace or dried flowers. Pomanders tend to shrink after a time but they maintain their fragrance for years.

Pomanders make lovely gifts

Rose petals add colour and fragrance to potpourri

HERBAL SACHETS

Fragrant herbal sachets can be hung in wardrobes, secreted among the undies in chests of drawers or hung in the airing cupboard. They make everything around them smell delicious and are excellent, inexpensive and thoughtful gifts. Always add a little dried lemon or orange peel to the sachet. This will help it to retain its perfume.

To make a sachet, cut two pieces of pretty cotton fabric into rectangles 20 cm x 11 cm. Turn right sides together and sew up, 1.5 cm from the outside edge, down one long side, across the bottom and up the second side, leaving 2 cm unsewn at the top. Turn down 0.5 cm from the top, press, then turn down a further 1.5 cm. Hand sew this edge down. Attach a small safety pin to the end of a 30 cm length of coloured ribbon and insert it through the casing. Pull the thread through the casing with the safety pin until it emerges at the other end. Turn the bag inside out. Now fill it with crumbled, dried herbs.

The following herbs are all suitable candidates for sachets: angelica, anise, basil, caraway, coriander, scented geraniums, lavender, lemon thyme, lemon verbena, mint, pot marjoram, rose, rosemary, thyme and violet.

MOTH BAGS

Certain herbs are known to repel moths, among them mint, rosemary, sage, southernwood, sweet basil and tansy. To protect winter woollies, make little drawstring herb bags, filled with crumbled dried herbs, and hang them on the hangers of clothes needing moth protection. Cover the garment with a polythene bag or keep the herb bags tucked among moth-prone jumpers.

Sage and rosemary can repel moths

GOURMET GIFTS

FINES HERBES
Sometimes in a recipe you will come across the term *fines herbes*. These are a mixture of chervil, chives, parsley, tarragon and occasionally lemon thyme, in equal proportions. If you grow these herbs in your garden, an airtight jar of *fines herbes* would make a beautiful gift for someone who loves cooking. They can be used fresh or dried but for the purposes of a gift, dried are more suitable. Parsley and chervil dry best in a warm oven while the other herbs can be dried in small bunches hung in the air. Chop the leaves and small stalks of the dried herbs finely. Mix them together well and fill an airtight pot or jar. Label and decorate with a ribbon. *Fines herbes* are traditionally used in egg, chicken and fish dishes, in salads, soups, sauces and even sandwiches. They are also delicious with lightly cooked vegetables.

BOUQUET GARNI

Bouquet garni is a small package of basic herbs, tied up in a cheesecloth bundle and dangled over the edge of casseroles and hotpots to give flavour to stews, soups and other 'wet' dishes. The three classic herbs are: parsley, bay leaf and thyme but sage, marjoram and rosemary are always a welcome addition and you can experiment with other herbs. Bouquets garnis are often added to a dish with a few pepperorns, a small carrot and a stalk of celery.

Basic Recipe

1 bay leaf
2 sprigs fresh parsley
1 sprig fresh thyme

Collect the herbs, dry and chop them. Mix together and put a little onto a square, 12 cm x 12 cm, of muslin or cheesecloth and gather up the corners. Tie up the bundle of herbs with a piece of string long enough to drop into the pot, leaving enough string over the edge for pulling out after cooking. A collection of half a dozen bouquets garnis, packed neatly into a box, could make an ideal gift for a gourmet.

CHERVIL
(*Anthriscus cerefolium*)

Plant description: Chervil is an attractive, hardy annual with fern-like leaves and small white flowers, that grows about 30 cm tall. It is not fussy about its soil, but likes regular watering, with sun in winter and dappled sun in summer. A short-lived herb, it self-seeds very easily, can be sown directly into the ground and is an ideal herb for growing indoors.

Uses: The delicate aniseed flavour of chopped chervil leaves can be best discovered in chervil soup. It also goes well with eggs, cheese, fish and lightly cooked vegetables. Chervil is an indispensible part of the *fines herbes* of French cooking. Do not, however, cook the leaves for any length of time, or their flavour will deteriorate.

Chervil poultices can reduce the swelling of bruises and its blood purifying properties are good for the kidneys. Also, it is said to ease gout and rheumatism if eaten daily. Some gardeners reckon that if chervil is grown close to radishes, it strengthens the radishes' hot flavour.

Chervil (Anthriscus cerefolium)

Parsley, thyme, bay leaves and peppercorns make the classic bouquet garni

There are a hundred and one ways to grow herbs — they are really very undemanding plants. Most need plenty of sun and well-drained soil. But you can grow some indoors, in pots or hanging baskets or massed together in different shaped containers on a patio or balcony.

They can flourish between pavers in the courtyard or peep from the brickwork of the barbecue area. Plant them in raised beds with the tallest growing erect and stately at the back or in the centre, and the smallest cascading down the sides. Some herbs make excellent border plants, while others that are tall and carry lovely flowers, can be mixed in with border flowers or added to a cottage garden. Herbs were always an integral part of the traditional cottage garden.

Many aromatic herbs made good edging plants along pathways, their scent drifting up as you brush past them. Lavender and eau-de-cologne mint are good examples of this. Rockeries are another sheltered spot for many herbs, though it is unwise to plant any that you cherish for their roots, as they are likely to be restricted in spread and hard to reach. If you have plenty of space you could design a formal herb garden based on traditional medieval or Elizabethan designs, which incorporated herbs grown for stewing and medicine as well as for flavour and perfume.

The important thing to remember is that your herbs must be accessible. When trekking out of your kitchen on a wet, dark night, you don't want to don a pair of wellies just to reach the parsley.

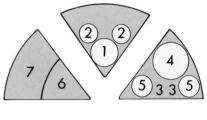

Herb garden intersected by paths. Suggested plantings are: 1 purple basil, 2 thyme, 3 chives, 4 dwarf rosemary, 5 sage, 6 mint in separate bed, 7 parsley, 8 marjoram, 9 shallots, 10 dill, 11 garlic

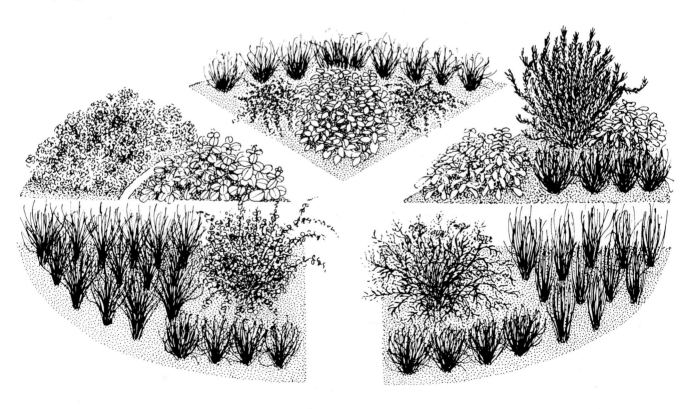

FORMAL HERB GARDENS

There are several traditional designs for formal herb gardens. The best known are the Knot, the Wheel, the Ladder and the Chequerboard.

THE KNOT GARDEN

A number of traditional shapes are used for growing beds of herbs but none is more intricate than the knot garden. As the name suggests, it consists of narrow, interlacing ribbon-like curves, each bed of herbs intersecting another bed of a different herb. Knot gardens were designed to be viewed from above, from the turrets, terraces or battlements of fine houses and castles. The work required to keep such a garden well-cared for today precludes many of us attempting this ambitious design but it is not really hard to do.

THE WHEEL

A well-loved shape is that of the wheel. Originally the different herbs were grown between the spokes of old cartwheels lain on their sides, the outer rim providing an edge. Today we can still grow our herbs in sections of a circle but with paving bricks or stones for spokes, so we can wander into the middle of the 'wheel' and reach any herb we want. A bird bath, sundial or statue in the centre of this herb garden adds an element of tranquility and old-fashioned charm to the garden. If there is room for a seat or bench, so much the better, for here will be a spot where you can soak up the peace and perfume of a timeless garden, away from the hurly-burly of twentieth-century life.

THE LADDER

The ladder is another formal shape often adopted for herb gardens. Herbs are grown in a rectangular bed with narrow footpaths along the sides and cutting across the bed to form 'rungs'. This bed shape is best suited to evergreen herbs that grow close to the ground.

CHEQUERBOARD

By missing out square pavers or bricks in a path and planting the square of soil with herbs, you can create a chequerboard effect. Variations on this pattern, with just the odd paver missing, provide a less formal arrangement. Use only low-growing herbs. Mint is ideal, as the pavers restrict its rampant root growth.

Formal herb garden, with lavender edged in box

PLANNING A HERB GARDEN

When planning a herb garden, first consider which herbs you are going to grow where. Some will grow very tall, like lovage, and should be planted where they will not overshadow sun-lovers. Some tend to creep out of control, like mint, and may need containing. Some, like borage, need plenty of sun, while others such as pennyroyal, can grow happily in semi-shade. Some are annuals, others biennials and still others perennials. Consult the Herb Calendar for each herb's special requirements and habits. Only when you have noted these will you be able to plan your herb garden so it works for you year in, year out. You may find it easiest to plot your herb garden by landscaping on paper first.

Where you decide to place your herbs depends on two very important factors. Firstly, nearly all herbs require full sun. Even most that can tolerate shade need full sun for a few hours each day. So position your herb garden with this in mind. Without sun, most herbs grow straggly and produce weak oils and flavour.

The second point to remember is that herbs need good drainage and no herb will put up with constantly wet roots. If your soil always becomes waterlogged after a downpour, drainage has to be improved before you can plant herbs there. If the soil is very heavy and clayey, you may need to dig a trench and lay down drainage pipes. This may seem a rather drastic measure but it is extremely effective if done properly and it means you won't have to worry further about drainage. Of course this only works if there is somewhere for the excess water to drain to. Alternatively, you may find it less trouble to build a raised herb bed — 30 cm is an adequate height.

To improve the quality of your soil, dig in plenty of river sand as deep as you can — half a metre if possible — and a good quantity of compost. If you are a little short on compost, add peat. Make sure you are breaking up the old, heavy topsoil and mixing it in well with the compost and sand. This should make a light, loose, nutritious soil that will support healthy, vigorous herbs.

When preparing your herb beds, an application of blood and bone is excellent natural fertiliser, conditioning the soil and giving perennial plants a good start. Dig in a couple of handfuls per square metre, with the river sand and compost. This extra food will pay dividends in the months to come and will preclude having to use other chemical fertilisers as top dressings, which may promote growth but not the flavour you want.

Most herbs like a slightly acid to slightly alkaline soil (pH 6.0 to 7.5; 7 is neutral, above 7 is alkaline). If you are growing healthy camellias, rhododendrons or azaleas, then you probably have a fairly acid soil. You can test this with a pH kit available from garden centres. To make the soil more alkaline, add dolomite, which is a natural mixture of magnesium carbonate and calcium carbonate. Scatter it lightly through the topsoil and fork in.

Even though many herbs can withstand dry conditions, they grow better and are more pungent when watered regularly. They can be watered morning or evening, and prefer a warm, moist soil throughout the day. Unlike many plants they can tolerate watering in full, hot sun. Always give them a good long drink until the soil is moist to about 30 cm deep.

Thyme seat in a herb garden

MAKING A GOOD COMPOST

Herbs love soil moderately enriched with compost. Even if you only have a small garden, it is possible to make good compost in a commercial or homemade bin. Keep a small plastic carton in the kitchen and throw all vegetable and animal waste into it, together with small quantities of torn up plain cardboard or wet, shredded newspaper. Each night empty the carton into your outdoor compost. Do not add the following: oil, fat, artificial fibres, many newspapers, any coloured or printed cardboards, plastic, kerosene, detergents, thick tree branches or stumps, weeds that are seeding or plants that are either diseased or have been treated with inorganic chemicals.

If you have space, a three-compartment compost bin is best. You can be filling one, while another is decomposing and you are using the finished product in the third. A height and width of 1.2 m is a good size for a compost bin.

It must have normal drainage, be near a water supply and be well aerated. You can add garden leaves, animal manure, grass clippings, bark, wood ash, seaweed, and all animal and vegetable waste to the compost. Make sure the mixture stays moist but not wet. Every so often sprinkle a handful of lime or dolomite over the heap. This counteracts the acid build-up in the compost and helps the decomposing process. Turn the heap regularly to aerate it. Composts are slower to decompose in winter than summer, as heat accelerates the process. Gradually (usually in 8–12 weeks) it will turn into a dark brown, moist, crumbly mixture, a rich plant food. From then on, you can apply it to the garden, either dug in or spread on top of the soil, to give it a new lease of life. In continuous rainy periods, protect the compost heap with a covering of polythene, wooden boards, or old carpet.

Comfrey (Symphytum officinale)

HERBS IN THE COMPOST
The application of certain herbs on a compost pile speeds up the breakdown of organic matter. Any one of the following will act as a magnificent activator, adding valuable elements to the mix and helping to eliminate any smell:

Chamomile: Even if you don't grow chamomile but only drink it as a tea, tip the used flower heads out of the teapot and onto the compost. They will improve any smell and also act as an activator, to accelerate the rate of decomposition and the absorption of calcium in the heap.

Comfrey: Comfrey can be rampant and will grow freely in the garden once it is established. If you have the room to grow it, scatter its leaves on the surface of every 20 cm high layer of compost. It will help to activate other organic elements to break down the heap quickly. It also adds a handsome sum of phosphorous, calcium, potassium and trace elements to the mix. The more comfrey you use, the better.

Dandelion: Do not be afraid to throw dandelions on the heap. The internal heat generated from the composting matter should be sufficient to kill off any seeds, while the leaves add calcium, iron and other minerals.

Nettle: Cut stinging nettles contribute iron to the heap and help to activate it.

Yarrow: Yarrow leaves cut up and dispersed in the compost can yield startling results: within a week the heap may be reduced to half its size or less. Even a small quantity of yarrow (3–4 leaves) seems to speed up the decaying process so fast it is hard to believe. A larger application seems to make no difference.

A HERBAL LIQUID FERTILISER
The Russian variety of comfrey makes the most excellent liquid fertiliser with a high potash content. Cut the leaves with a pair of shears and steep them in enough hot water to cover them. Leave for 24 hours. Bottle in a screw-top, airtight container and use diluted with water in the ratio of 1:10 leaves to water.

German chamomile (Matricaria chamomilla)

MINT AND TARRAGON
Mint and tarragon are greedy for space. Plant them away from your other herbs, if possible, and keep an eye on their territorial ambitions.

Yarrow (Achillea millefolium *var.* Rosea)

BUYING HERBS — SEEDS OR SEEDLINGS?

Many herbs — such as basil, dill, nasturtium, parsley and chives — are easy to raise from seed, but they do need regular attention. You will have to wait at least six weeks and usually longer (up to a year for chives), before you can begin snipping them.

Some herbs are more trouble than others to grow from seed: parsley can take six weeks or more to germinate, French tarragon often doesn't set seed and is usually grown from cuttings, and others, like dill, dislike transplanting but can be sown direct into the garden and later thinned out.

POT LUCK

The satisfaction is just as great if you opt to start with seedlings. Very often a single pot of herbs that you plan to use consistently throughout the season is not enough for your requirements. If you have a pot of tarragon, a couple of stems will not see you through many dishes of Chicken Tarragon. So unless pots are large and overflowing with herbs, buy two or three plants of any one kind. They will also look more impressive in the garden than a lone plant.

When buying herbs in pots, always choose the most robust and sturdy plants. Containers planted with several types of herbs in the garden centre may look very pretty but if the herbs need different conditions, they won't look good for too long. It may be necessary to transplant each one according to its requirements when you get it home.

If possible, you should not leave seedlings in a hot car for long. If it is unavoidable, leave the windows slightly open. Any plant is liable to wilt in such hot conditions and although recovery is usual with a good watering, it cannot be guaranteed.

Many nursery potting mixes these days are sawdust-based and do not provide much nutrition for a growing plant, so transplant the herbs, even if you plan to keep them in pots.

Some herbs are easier to grow from seedlings, and are readily available from local nurseries, and nurseries specialising in herbs

To grow a herb like cress from seed, sprinkle seeds on damp tissue paper

Cress shoots appear after 2 days

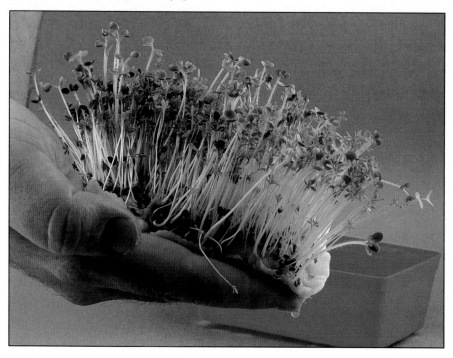

Cress shoots after 3 days

78

RAISING HERBS FROM SEED

Sowing in seed trays is likely to be more successful than sowing directly into the open ground as conditions can be more easily controlled, particularly when sowing perennial herbs which are slower growing than annuals. Use punnets, small plastic pots, or ice cream and margarine containers with holes punched into the bottom, for drainage. Peat or fibre pots are biodegradable and can be planted out along with the seedling herb. Mix up a seed compost of one part peat, one part good quality sand loam and one part river sand, with a sprinkling of blood and bone; or buy a seed-raising compost.

Fill the containers to within 2 cm of the top of each rim. Snip one corner of the seed packet and open it carefully. Gently sprinkle a few seeds over the seed compost. Add a light sprinkling of compost over the top of the seeds, to about twice the seeds' depth. Firm down with a matchbox or flat board.

Then place the containers in a sink of water, shallow enough to avoid water overflowing into the container but sufficient to seep into the soil through the drainage holes in the base of each container. When the top of the compost is damp, lift out the containers and leave them to drain. Stretch a piece of clear plastic wrap over each container. Leave trays in a sheltered, airy position, where you can keep an eye on them. Keep the mix moist and lift the plastic each night to discourage fungal problems.

Some seedlings may spring up in a week or so; others, like parsley, can take six weeks or more. Once you have shoots, remove the plastic entirely. When the seedlings have developed about four leaves and a small root system, it is time to transplant them from the seedbox into either the open ground or containers.

If you are transplanting into pots, fill the pot to within 2 cm of the rim with potting mix. Poke your finger into the mix and drop the seedling gently into the hole, ensuring no damage is done to the root. Press the mix gently around the seedling and top up with potting mix. Depending on the size of the pot, pop in as many seedlings as there will be room for fully grown plants. A pot of grown herbs should look filled and generous without being crowded.

To transplant into the open ground, the soil should be prepared. Gently lift out each seedling with the soil around its roots. Make a small hole in the ground, either with your finger or with a dibbler. Just big enough to take the seedling. Pop

Packets of herb seeds are usually available from local suburban nurseries

it into the hole and press the surrounding soil firmly but gently around the seedling. Do likewise with the other seedlings, leaving enough space for each plant to grow to its full potential. Water the new seedlings in, to settle the soil around them and encourage root growth.

Keep a vigilant eye on them each day, watering them regularly in hot weather. Remove any weeds that grow up around the seedlings — they will steal valuable resources.

Once the plants are well established, lightly cultivate around them, uprooting the weeds and aerating the soil. Before summer arrives, mulch to keep down weeds and maintain moisture in the soil.

Preparing a seed bed

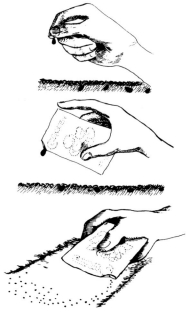

Seeds can be sown directly from the seed packet, taking care to space out seeds. Small seeds can be shaken out to ensure even distribution. Large seeds can be tapped individually into the soil directly from the packets.

To produce level soil or spread fertiliser evenly, make a simple spreader at home. Use a piece of hardwood about 1000 mm long × 100 mm × 25 mm, a rake handle, some wire and nails. Plane off one edge of the hardwood. Bore a hole halfway through to take the wire. Nail the handle in place on the leveller-head. Guy it by threading wire through the holes to the handle.

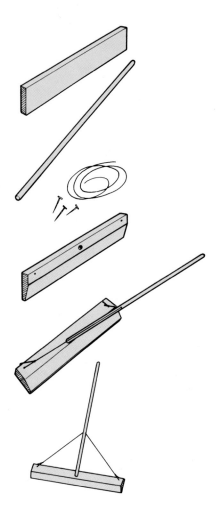

When the second pair of true leaves have developed on a young plant, seedlings can be transplanted either for thinning out or planting direct into the garden.

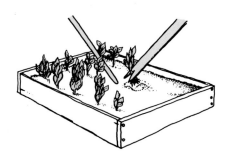

HERB CALENDAR

COMMON NAME	SYNONYMS	BOTANICAL NAME
Angelica		*Archangelica officinalis* or *Angelica archangelica*
Anise	sweet alice, sweet cummin	*Pimpinella anisum*
Basil	includes sweet basil; bush basil	*Ocymum basilicum* *O. minimum*
Bay	Grecian, Roman, noble or royal laurel, sweet bay	*Laurus nobilis*
Bergamot	bee balm, Oswego tea	*Monarda didyma*
Caraway		*Carum carvi*
Catmint	catnip, catnep, field balm	*Nepeta cataria*
Chamomile	Roman, garden or low chamomile; German or wild chamomile	*Matricaria chamomilla* *Anthemis nobilis*
Chervil	French parsley, salad chervil	*Anthriscus cerefolium*
Chicory	wild chicory, succory, wild succory	*Cichorium intybus*
Chives	includes garlic and onion chives	*Allium schoenoprasum*
Coriander	Chinese parsley, cilantro	*Coriandrum sativum*
Dill	dilly, garden dill	*Anethum graveolens*
Fennel	common or wild fennel	*Foeniculum vulgare*
Garlic		*Allium sativum*
Geraniums, scented	includes rose; peppermint; coconut; lemon	*Pelargonium graveolens* *P. tomentosum* *P. enossularoides* *P. limonium*
Ginger	African or black ginger	*Zingiber officinale*

GROWTH HABITS	PROPAGATION
biennial to 2m, umbrella-like clusters of green-white flowers, semi-shade, moist soil	seeds in punnets spring to summer, transplant when 10 cm tall, space 100 cm apart
annual to 60 cm, white flowers and feathery leaves, full sun, well-drained, needs wind protection	seeds direct spring or autumn, 30 cm apart
annual 15–60 cm, small white flowers and shiny oval leaves, full sun or semi-shade, moist rich soil	seeds direct late spring or early summer, 15–30 cm apart
evergreen tree to 11 m, white flowers and purple-black fruits, full sun or semi-shade, moist well-drained soil, not frost resistant	very slow growing; plant well-established tree in pot or ground
perennial to 1.2 m, attractive lavender, pink or scarlet flowers, morning sun or semi-shade, moist rich soil	root divisions any time of year or seeds in spring, 15 cm apart
biennial to 60 cm, fine lacy leaves and umbrella-like clusters of white flowers, full sun, well-drained soil, needs wind protection	seeds direct spring or autumn, 20 cm apart, thin out
perennial to 1.6 m, pointed scalloped leaves and white flowers with purple spots, full sun or semi-shade, well-drained soil	seeds, cuttings or root divisions in spring, summer or autumn respectively
perennial to 30 cm, white or yellow flowers, full sun, any soil; annual to 45 cm, similar flowers to Roman chamomile, full sun, any soil	tip cuttings any time of year; seeds or root division
annual to 50 cm, finely cut leaves like parsley and clusters of white flowers, semi-shade, moist rich soil	seeds direct spring or autumn, 10 cm apart
perennial to 1.5 m, blue or violet flowers, full sun, rich soil	seeds direct in spring, 45 cm apart
perennial to 20 cm, long thin strap-like leaves and purple flowers, moist rich soil, sun or semi shade	seeds direct or plant bulb divisions, spring, summer or autumn, 20 cm apart
annual to 60 cm, parsley-like leaves and pink-white flowers, full sun, light soil, protect from winds	seeds direct spring or early summer, 30 cm apart, thin out
annual to 90 cm, fern-like leaves and attractive yellow flowers, full sun, well-drained rich soil	seeds direct spring, summer or autumn, in clumps, 30 cm apart
perennial to 1.5 m, feathery leaves and yellow flowers, full sun, rich well-drained soil, protect from winds	seeds direct late spring or early summer, 20 cm apart, thin out
perennial to 1 m, flat strap-like leaves and mauve-white flowers, full sun, well-drained rich soil	bulbs in spring or autumn, 25 mm deep, 15 cm apart
perennial to 1 m, large frilled leaves, pink flowers trailing perennial to 30 cm, small white flowers perennial to 30 cm, small pink flowers perennial to 1.5 m, small white flowers all require full sun or semi-shade, well-drained soil	root or tip cuttings in late summer
perennial to 1.5 m, spikes of white and purple flowers, semi-shade well-drained soil with lime	root pieces in late spring, 3 cm below surface

Horseradish		*Cochlearia armoracia*
Lavender	**includes English;** **French;** **Italian/Spanish**	*Lavandula vera, L. officinalis* or *L. spica* *L. dentata* *L. stoechas*
Lemon balm	**balm, bee, blue or sweet balm,** **melissa**	*Melissa officinalis*
Lemon grass		*Cymbopogon citratus*
Lovage	**European lovage, lavose, sea** **parsley**	*Levisticum officinale*
Marjoram	**includes garden, knotted, and sweet** **marjoram**	*Origanum majorana*
Mint	**includes common mint (spearmint);** **applemint;** **peppermint;** **pennyroyal**	*Mentha spicata* *M. rotundifolia* or *M. suaveolens* *M. piperita* *M. pulegium*
Nasturtium	**Indian or large Indian cress**	*Tropaeolum majus*
Oregano	**wild marjoram**	*Origanum vulgare*
Parsley	**includes Hamburg, Italian (flat-** **leaved) and curly-leaved (common or** **garden) parsley**	*Petroselinum crispum*
Rosemary	**includes ordinary rosemary and** **prostrate rosemary**	*Rosmarinus officinalis*
Sage	**garden sage**	*Salvia officinalis*
Savoury	**includes summer savoury;** **winter savoury**	*Satureia hortensis* *S. montana*
Sorrel	**common, garden or meadow sorrel,** **sourgrass**	*Rumex acetosa*
Tarragon	**estragon, includes Russian and** **French**	*Artemisia dracunculus*
Thymes	**includes common or garden thyme,** **lemon thyme**	*Thymus vulgaris* *T. citriodorus*
Watercress	**scurvy grass, tall nasturtium**	*Nasturtium officinale*

perennial to 1 m, rosettes of dark green leaves like spinach and tiny white flowers, semi-shade, moist rich soil	root pieces 15 cm long, plant horizontally 30 cm apart cover with 5 cm soil, roots harvested 6–7 months later
perennial to 1 m, silvery grey leaves and classic spikes of blue-purple flowers perennial to 1 m, small lavender flowers perennial to 30 cm, deep purple flowers, many varieties of lavender available, with white, pink, green, blue, and purple flowers, full sun, rich well-drained soil	seeds in punnets or cuttings, spring or autumn
perennial to 90 cm, mint-like leaves and inconspicuous white, pink or blue flowers, full sun or semi-shade, moist rich soil	root division, stem cuttings or sow seeds direct 60 cm apart
perennial to 2 m, long slender leaves, full sun, rich soil	plant division
perennial to 2 m, dark green celery-like leaves and white or yellow flowers, sun or semi-shade, moist rich soil, protect from winds	seeds direct spring or autumn, 60 cm apart
perennial 25–75 cm, small oval leaves and white or purple flowers, full sun light, well-drained soil	seeds, cuttings and root divisions late spring or early summer, 30 cm apart
perennial to 60 cm, white flowers perennial to 1.5 m, mauve flowers perennial to 90 cm, pinky mauve flowers perennial to 15 cm, mauve flowers all the mints prefer semi-shade, but some will grow in sun, moist rich soil	root divisions, cuttings and seeds any time of year, best in large pots to contain spreading roots
climbing or sprawling annual, pretty round leaves and flowers in red, yellow and orange, full sun, any soil	seeds or root division in spring
perennial to 75 cm, tiny purple flowers, parent plant of marjoram, similar growth habits	see *Marjoram*
biennial 15–60 cm, flat or curly leaves and yellow flowers, full sun or shade, moist well-drained soil see Mint	seeds direct in spring, summer or autumn, 20 cm apart
evergreen perennial 20–150 cm, grey-green narrow leaves and attractive blue flowers, full sun or semi-shade, rich well-drained soil	seeds or cuttings in spring, summer or autumn, 100 cm apart
perennial to 60 cm, grey-green leaves and purple flowers, full sun, alkaline soil	seeds or cuttings in late summer or autumn, 30 cm apart
annual to 60 cm, bronze-green leaves and pink flowers, full sun, light soil; perennial to 40 cm, semi-prostrate rounded leaves and white or lavender flowers, full sun, light sandy soil	seeds direct in spring and summer, 15 cm apart; seeds or cuttings in autumn, 30 cm apart
perennial to 90 cm, big flat heart-shaped leaves, full sun, moist rich soil	seeds direct or root division in spring or autumn, 15 cm apart, divide established plants
perennial to 1 m, Russian has rough light green leaves, French has dark slender leaves with small white or yellow flowers, full sun, light well-drained soil, protect from winds	cuttings or seeds in spring or summer, 60 cm apart
perennial to 30 cm, exquisitely pretty white, pink or purple flowers; perennial to 30 cm, tiny white flowers, silver and gold leaved varieties available, all thymes need full sun, well-drained poor soil	seeds, cuttings, root divisions in spring or autumn, 15 cm apart
perennial to 45 cm, dark green fleshy leaves and small white flowers, semi-shade, moist soil preferably near water	cuttings or seeds direct in spring

PLANTING OUT POTTED HERBS

If you plan to plant our your herbs, prepare the bed first (see pages 76 ff) and water the plant some hours before transplanting. With the fingers of one hand gently gripping the main stems of the herb, invert the pot and tap it firmly on the bottom and against the sides. The entire herb and root ball should drop out in one piece. If you have difficulty in dislodging it, then soak the plant in warm water for a few minutes and drain, before trying again.

Dig a suitable-sized hole for the herb with a trowel. Gently straighten out any curling roots, loosen the earth from around root tips, taking care not to damage any, then place the root ball into the hole. Position it correctly, make sure it isn't leaning over and is planted at the exact height it was planted in the pot. Very often the plant looks more attractive from one angle rather than another, so experiment a little. Once in position, fill in the hole with soil all around. Firm in the plant and give it a good drink. Keep an eye on it for the next few days, making sure it does not lack water, and mulch around the herbs before hot weather arrives.

A WORD ON WORMS
The lowly earthworm is extremely good news to the gardener. Its presence is an indication of good quality soil. Worms feed happily on decaying organic matter such as rotting vegetation, dead animals or manure. Their special digestive system breaks down the food to make highly nutritious deposits in the soil. These deposits are rich in nitrogen, phosphorus, potassium, magnesium and other minerals, so treasure your worms and do nothing to harm them — they are most efficient recyclers.

PROPAGATION

The best time for dividing perennials is in autumn and winter, though early spring is also possible. Woody-stemmed herbs can be propagated from softwood cuttings in early summer.

There is a third method of propagation called layering, which works with a surprising number of herbs. It is usually most effective during the greatest growth activity.

LAYERING
Suitable candidates are scented geranium, lemon balm, all mints, white horehound, marjoram, hyssop, rosemary (slow), sage, savory and thymes. Plants often propagate themselves by layering. One stem of the plant straying across the soil often starts to put down roots in a certain spot. You can encourage this by taking one or two stems and gently securing them to the ground with a hairpin or small U-shaped piece of wire. Water this spot liberally and eventually the plant will put down roots. About six weeks after it has rooted, you can cut the connecting stem. You now have a completely independent plant that can be moved to another part of the garden.

Above: The correct way to take a cutting
Below: To pot cuttings, dibble a hole in prepared potting mix, and insert the cutting, firming the soil around to stand the cutting upright

CUTTING

Most herbs can be propagated from cuttings except those that grow in clumps e.g. dandelion, borage, comfrey, lemon grass and horseradish, but this method is most useful with woody-stemmed herbs.

Cuttings are best taken after flowering. Take stems that are firm and healthy, with a woody heel if possible, and trim off the bottom leaves. Put the cuttings in a seed-raising mix and water them well. Dipping the bases in hormone rooting powder can increase your chances of success. Check the date on the powder as it is only effective for a certain time. Spray the leaves regularly with water and never allow the soil to completely dry out.

To maintain the moisture in the soil, you can cover the container of cuttings with transparent plastic, glass or cling wrap but remember to air your cuttings at least every 24 hours. Leave the cuttings in a sheltered warm spot out of direct sunlight.

When cuttings show new growth, you know they have rooted successfully. Wait a further two weeks or so before transplanting cuttings into containers or open ground. Softwood cuttings usually take a few weeks to strike; hardwood cuttings can take as long as six months.

ROOT DIVISION

This is an easy way of multiplying your stock of perennial herbs, provided you have a healthy, well-rooted plant in the first place. Simply dig up your existing plant or turn it out of its pot. Remove surrounding soil and cut or pull the root apart. Repot or replant each section as a separate plant. This is best done just before or early in the growing season, as new growth is beginning. It is not always necessary to dig up the entire plant. If dividing strongly growing plants in summer or autumn, you may need to trim foliage to compensate for root interference.

A good root system has developed on this rosemary cutting

Pennyroyal being prepared for root division

PRUNING

At the end of the growing year, woody-stemmed herbs, such as lavender and rosemary, should be cut back to maintain a good shape for the next year's growth. With lavender, prune spent flowers, taking 3–4 cm of leafy stem (more for large lavenders). With rosemary, pinch prune when young and never prune back into bare stems.

Herbs grown for their leaves will receive regular harvesting anyway. Plants that grow out of hand, for example, thyme or mint, can be cut back periodically to keep them compact.

If you are growing a herb for the flavour, perfume or efficacy of its leaves, you should discourage flowering. When the flowers appear, snip them off. This will concentrate the plant's energy in the leaves instead of the flowers.

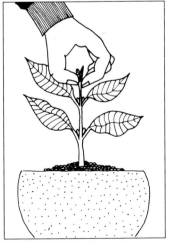

To prune pot plants, pinch out the top sets of leaves and shoots from leaf axils

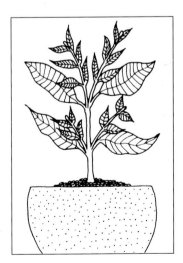

A compact bushy shape results

85

HERBAL PESTICIDES

PEST	HERBS
Ants	Tansy, pennyroyal, spearmint, peppermint. Even dried, these are effective in and out of the house.
Aphids	Nasturtiums, pennyroyal.
Borers	Nasturtiums, garlic.
Fleas	Catnip rubbed into dog or cat fur can be effective. Fennel and wormwood also repel fleas.
Cutworm	These are the grubs of a nocturnal moth which cause considerable damage to green stems very fast; tansy is a good repellant.
Flies	Basil, tansy, chamomile, wormwood all work in or out of the house.
Grasshoppers	An infusion of chillies, capsicum and onion in water, left for a day, will act as a very effective grasshopper spray.
Mice	Catnip and spearmint.
Mosquitoes	Basil, mint, chamomile, southernwood, tansy. Rub yourself with the leaves for a natural Aeroguard.
Clothes moths	Fill sachets with dried mint, lavender, sage, wormwood, southernwood, santolina or rosemary and place in drawers and wardrobes.
Red spider mites	Coriander, lemon grass.
Cabbage moth and cabbage butterfly	Hyssop, mint, rosemary.
Silverfish	Rosemary.
Cats and dogs	Rue planted as a border around flower beds.

Above: Wormwood (Artemesia absinthium)

Right: Tansy (Tanacetum vulgare)

Housefly (Musca domestica)

PEST CONTROL

Since herbs are generally grown to be eaten, organic methods of pest control are best. Inorganic sprays, apart from being toxic, can also destroy useful wildlife in the garden, such as bees and earthworms.

NATURAL PREDATORS
Some animals in the garden are natural predators of larvae and plant-loving insects, so cherish these. Among the most effective are frogs, lizards, most spiders, most ladybirds, lacewings, hoverflies and praying mantises.

HAND REMOVAL
Large and slow insects may be plucked off plants by hand.

PLANTING
Some herbs repel insects, others attract them. Grown close to prized favourities, special herbs can be used effectively to control insects. For a list of these useful herbs, see our table, *Herbal Pesticides*.

Above: Alpine grasshopper

Catmint (Nepeta species)

Above: Ants forming a nest

Above: Cutworm (Arctotis species)

COMPANION PLANTING

Besides the efficacious effects of herbs in compost and their usefulness in natural pest and fungi control sprays, herbs can also be good for the garden in another way. By growing specific herbs and others plants together, it has been found that the association can be mutually beneficial.

Companion planting, or allelopathy as it is scientifically known, is both an art and a science. To know which plants are happiest growing together we have compiled a chart. Many of these discoveries have been stumbled upon by gardeners and passed on by word of mouth. Some strange bedfellows remain scientifically unexplained and yet they seem to work. You may discover new successful partnerships yourself.

Try planting a few herbs near a group of companion plants; e.g. three basil plants could be planted beside or within a bed of asparagus or tomatoes.

You can also use a variety of herbs as attractive and beneficial edging or border plants; e.g. a bed of cabbage could be edged with oregano, dill, chamomile, coriander, mint, rosemary, sage and thyme. Variety can help to reduce pests and diseases.

HERBS	GOOD COMPANIONS	BAD COMPANIONS
Anise	coriander	—
Basil	tomatoes, asparagus	rue
Bee balm	tomatoes	—
Borage	strawberries, tomatoes, squash	—
Caraway	peas	fennel
Chamomile	onions, cabbage, broccoli, peppermint	—
Chervil	carrots, radishes, dill	—
Chives	carrots, apple and other fruit trees, roses, parsley	—
Comfrey	most vegetable crops	—
Coriander	carrots, cabbage, anise	fennel
Dandelion	fruit trees	—
Dill	cabbage, corn, lettuce, cucumber, broccoli, onions, carrots	fennel
Fennel	—	beans, caraway, dill, tomatoes, kohlrabi, wormwood
Foxgloves	improve storage quality of potatoes, tomatoes and apples	—
Garlic	roses, fruit trees, raspberries, tomatoes	peas, beans, cabbage, strawberries
Horseradish	potatoes, fruit trees	—
Hyssop	grapes, cabbage, Brussels sprouts, most vegetable crops	radishes
Lemon balm	tomatoes, most vegetable crops	—
Lovage	vegetable crops	—
Marigolds	French beans, potatoes, corn, tomatoes, fruit trees	—
Marjoram	vegetable crops	—
Mint	cabbage family, tomatoes	parsley

Above: Chives in flower (Allium schoenoprasum)

Right: Coriander flowers (Coriandrum sativum)

Nasturtium	radishes, potatoes, fruit trees, broccoli, cabbage, squash, pumpkin, tomatoes, cucumber	—
Oregano	broccoli, cabbage, cauliflower, cucumber, grapes	—
Parsley	beans, chives, roses, tomatoes, asparagus, carrots, turnips	mint
Pennyroyal	broccoli, Brussels sprouts, cabbage	—
Peppermint	cabbage, chamomile	—
Pyrethrum	strawberries	—
Rosemary	sage, carrots, cabbage family, beans	potatoes, rue
Rue	fig trees, roses other shrubs and trees	sage, basil, rosemary
Sage	rosemary, cabbage family, carrots, peas, beans	rue, cucumber
Salad burnet	thyme, mint	—
Savory, summer	onions, beans	—
Southernwood	cabbages, fruit trees	—
Stinging nettles	currant bushes, soft fruits, tomatoes, most herbs	—
Tansy	fruit trees, roses, cabbage family, raspberries, blackberries, most soft fruits, grapes	—
Tarragon	all-purpose garden helper	—
Thyme	cabbage	—
Valerian	vegetable crops	—
Yarrow	vegetable and herb crops	—

Above: Lemon balm (Melissa officinalis)

Above: Rosemary in flower (Rosmarinus officinalis)

Above: Tansy (Tanecetum vulgare)

Right: Comfrey in an urn (Symphytum officinale)

CONTAINER CLUES

Anyone with a balcony, courtyard or small backyard can grow a splendid array of herbs in a comparatively small space by using a variety of containers. If you want to grow some of the deeply-rooted herbs, however, like horseradish, you will have to build a raised bed or find an extremely deep pot. Very tall herbs, like lovage, are not really suitable for pots.

Window boxes, hanging baskets, urns, pots or old sinks can all be made suitable homes for herbs and there are a number of proprietary potting mixes that provide adequate soil — though some may not be very nutritious for any length of time. For this reason you may wish to mix your own. Remember, containers are very prone to drying out in the midday sun and this can be fatal for small herbs. Peat, once dried out, is difficult to moisten again, so use a mix of four parts crumbly, top-quality loam, two parts moist peatmoss and compost and two parts coarse river sand. The mix will be rather heavy: so if you intend to move the pots around the garden, choose smallish ones and don't use large hanging baskets as their weight, when wet, may strain their fastenings.

Raise containers on bricks or supports that will provide good air circulation around the pot. Watch your herbs very carefully through the hot summer months to make sure they don't dry out. Test with a finger 2.5 cm into the compost and if it feels dry, the plants need watering — this may be necessary twice a day in the height of summer. Hanging baskets are particularly prone to drying out and are easily forgotten. Always line the basket with sphagnum moss, plastic, bark, or special fibre available from garden centres.

Unlike herbs in well-prepared open ground, herbs in containers do need feeding. During the growing season liquid feed plants every two weeks. Nothing is required in winter.

Below: Strawberry pot of herbs, basil, parsley, feverfew and tansy

Lorna Rose

REPOTTING
The best time for most herbs to be repotted is spring. Some can be potted up in autumn and rest quite contentedly through to the next spring when they will burst into life.

Wash pots in warm, soapy water or disinfectant with a wire brush before use. This ensures the pot is not holding any damaging microbes or spores.

To prevent clogging over the pot's drainage holes, cover them with broken clay pot pieces (crocks) or gravel. Add a little potting mix before tapping out the herb from its previous pot. If the plant is root-bound and won't budge, sink the pot in warm water for a couple of minutes.

To tap out the plant, place two fingers of one hand around the stem of the plant, then carefully invert the pot and gently tap its bottom and sides with your other hand. The plant should slip out complete

Weldon Trannies

*Above: Herbs in a strawberry pot —
chives, parsley and sage*

GIFTS FOR THE GARDENER

A POT OF HERBS

An obvious and valuable gift often not thought of, is perhaps the simplest and most practical of all — a pot of herbs, raised yourself from seed. You really can't lose with this one. Many people love plants, and a useful plant is even better.

Choose a pretty and practical shaped pot and make sure the soil is correctly prepared. Buy some tall plastic labels from the garden centre, and an indelible marker. Write the herb's common name and its botanical Latin name on the label and push it into the soil. If you have doubts about your recipient's gardening ability, perhaps write a few simple notes on how to look after it. Choose a herb which suits the needs of the person to whom you are giving it. For example, if the recipient lives in an apartment, it is no use giving lovage or chervil. A more thoughtful gift would be a pot of marjoram, thyme, mint or parsley to put on the kitchen windowsill. If the recipient has a flea-ridden dog, a pot of pennyroyal might be appreciated; or give a container full of basil to someone who loves eating tomatoes.

Why not put several herbs together in a pot? Make sure the herbs all like the same conditions, or some of them will not live very long. For a final touch, wrap up the pot in festive paper and tie it with a big ribbon.

Lorna Rose

with soil ball. If possible, gently tease out the root tips but do not damage them.

Sit the plant on the fresh potting mix in the new pot and add as much mix as you need to raise the plant to within 2 cm of the pot rim. Then fill in the edges around the plant, firm down and add any extra mix to make level. Give the herb a long drink. Place it in a shady place for a couple of days to let it acclimatise, then move it into the sun (unless it is a shade-lover).

STRAWBERRY POTS

Herbs tumbling out of the pocket openings of these terracotta urns look lovely but the secret to their success lies in the types of herbs used and the method of planting. In the top, most low or medium-height herbs can be planted, but in the pockets you will need a bushy creeping

Above: An entire herb garden can be grown in pots; even quite large plants, like the lavenders, will thrive

plant and probably the most suitable is thyme.

The way to plant is to fill the pot as you would any other, up to the first pocket. Sink the roots of the first thyme plant into the soil from the inside and poke only the leaves out of the pocket. Firm down the roots in the soil. Then fill up the urn with potting mix to the next pocket and repeat the process. Continue like this until you reach the top. If you fill up the urn first and insert the plants into the pockets from the outside, you will find they may be dislodged during the first good watering. Water slowly, making sure the water penetrates the potting mix, and does not just run out of the pockets.

THE KITCHEN GARDEN INDOORS

Everyone can enjoy a kitchen garden. If you live in a flat or unit, in addition to using window boxes, hanging baskets or balcony pots, you can grow many herbs indoors provided they have good conditions.

Most important of these is direct sunlight and fresh air. If you have a warm, sunny windowsill, at least for half the day, or a sunroom, your herbs will be happy, although in summer, leaves sometimes scorch in the middle of the day and the plant has to be moved. Try to maintain an even room temperature. Herbs don't respond well to extreme temperature changes.

Don't attempt to grow very tall or deeply-rooted herbs: the best candidates are marjoram, basil, rosemary, chervil, thyme, winter savory, lemon balm, chives and parsley. All of these are useful culinary herbs. If your sunny spot is in the kitchen, so much the better. You will be able to snip at them as you cook. In fact, chervil seems to thrive better in the winter inside than out. Basil, too, is unlikely to survive in the garden through winter except in warm climates, but can be sown from seed, in summer to early autumn, for indoor pots to take you through the winter. Bush basil is easiest to grow in pots.

To make a suitable potting soil for herbs, use one part river sand with one part peat and well-rotted compost or leafmould, and one part good quality loam. Leave the mixture for a couple of days before planting. A simple alternative is a good, ready-made potting mixture.

Use any containers you like — terracotta, plastic or stone pots; tin, china, or wooden containers — but whatever you choose must have adequate drainage holes in the bottom. Watering indoor plants is a tricky business. Over-watering leads to sodden roots, something herbs hate, while insufficient watering results in poor growth. Poor soil conditions mean plants will have a weak flavour and lose their effectiveness. The best way to ensure that you are watering correctly is to place your pots of herbs in a tray of gravel. If you overwater by mistake, the tray will take up the excess and it will evaporate into the surrounding air,

keeping it humid which herbs appreciate. Whatever you do, don't leave herbs standing in saucers of water for any length of time.

Most plants, including herbs, prefer water at room temperature rather than straight from the tap, so leave water to stand for an hour if possible before pouring. Water from the top and fine-spray the leaves occasionally to remove any dust.

Herbs need good air circulation. If

Above: Vietnamese mint is not a true mint, but a Polyganum species

Below: Marjoram and thyme growing in pots, surrounded by flowers

cigarette smoke and other fumes have made the air stuffy, plants will enjoy being put outside on warm, sunny days to refresh themselves. Even on rainy days, thirsty plants will welcome a good soak. Pure rainwater is better than tapwater. If you can't put pots outside, open the window on days when there is no wind — they dislike draughts. Also, turn pots around at regular intervals so that plants don't grow lop-sided.

Although fertilising is unnecessary for outdoor plants, indoor herbs do need feeding. Regular applications of organic plant food should be given about every two weeks during the growing season.

If possible herbs should be planted out in the garden after one year. If this can't be done, then at least replace the soil, and use a pot one size larger. Plants surrounded by so little soil quickly exhaust nutrients and cease to flourish.

SPROUTING SEEDS
You would be surprised how easy it is to encourage many seeds to burst into life on your kitchen windowsill. Here are just a few: fenugreek, alfalfa, fennel, mung beans, wheatgrass, all delicious and valuable nutrition.

Buy a few fresh seeds at a time and scatter them in a glass container. Pour in cold water and, with your hand over the top, agitate the seeds and water for 30 seconds. Cover the top with a piece of muslin or cheesecloth and secure with an elastic band. Tip the water out of the container, catching the seeds in the cloth. Leave the container upside-down to drain for a few minutes. Then place it in a warm, airy spot, away from direct sunlight and wait for the magic. In winter, seeds may take 4–5 days to germinate but in summer results are much faster. The seeds should be rinsed and well drained each day to keep them fresh. You can also buy special growing dishes for sprouting seeds.

These little sprouting seeds are packed with goodness. They contain high levels of life-giving minerals, proteins and, once the first two seed leaves appear, vitamin C. Sprouts should be eaten within 24 hours of the green shoots appearing. If left too long, sprouts tend to rot. They are best eaten raw in salads or sandwiches.

Above: Herb garden in pots

FOR YOUR INFORMATION

EQUIVALENT TERMS

AUSTRALIA	UK	USA
Equipment and terms		
can	tin	can
crushed	minced	pressed
frying pan	frying pan	skillet
grill	grill	broil
greaseproof paper	greaseproof paper	waxproof paper
paper cases	paper baking cases	baking cups
paper towel	kitchen paper	white paper towel
plastic wrap	cling film	plastic wrap
seeded	stoned	pitted
Swiss roll tin	Swiss roll tin	jelly roll pan
Ingredients		
bacon rasher	bacon rasher	bacon slice
beetroot	beetroot	beets
bicarbonate of soda	bicarbonate of soda	baking soda
black olive	black olive	ripe olive
calamari	squid	calamari
capsicum	pepper	sweet pepper
cornflour	cornflour	cornstarch
cream	single cream	light or coffee cream
eggplant	aubergine	eggplant
essence	essence	extract
plain flour	plain flour	all-purpose flour
green cabbage	white or roundhead cabbage	cabbage
icing sugar	icing sugar	confectioners' sugar
pawpaw	pawpaw	papaya or papaw
pimiento	red pepper	pimiento
prawn	prawn or shrimp	shrimp
red onion	Spanish onion	Bermuda onion
self-raising flour	self raising flour	all-purpose flour with baking powder, 1 cup:2 teaspoons
shallot	spring onion	scallion
snow pea	mangetout, sugar pea	snow pea
stock cube	stock cube	bouillon cube
stringless green bean	whole French bean	stringed green bean
sultanas	sultanas	seedless white or golden raisins
tasty cheese	mature Cheddar	Cheddar
rich cream	double cream	heavy or whipping cream
tomato puree	tomato puree	tomato paste
tomato sauce	tomato sauce	tomato ketchup
unsalted butter	unsalted butter	sweet butter
wholemeal flour	wholemeal flour	wholewheat flour
yoghurt	natural yoghurt	unflavoured yoghurt
young pea	petit pols	sweet pea
zucchini	courgette	zucchini

Oven Temperatures

	Celsius	Fahrenheit
Very slow	120	250
Slow	140–150	275–300
Moderately slow	160	325
Moderate	180	350
Moderately hot	190	375
Hot	200	400
	220	425
	230	450
Very hot	250–280	475–500

Measurements

Standard Metric Measures

1 cup	=	250 mL
1 tablespoon	=	20 mL
1 teaspoon	=	5 mL

All spoon measurements are level

If you need to substitute

FRESH FRUIT: replace with canned or tinned fruit.

FRESH HERBS: replace with a quarter of the recommended quantity, using dried herbs.

LEBANESE CUCUMBER: Also called English or Telegraph cucumber; replace with any smooth-skinned cucumber.

LING: replace with haddock, hake or cod.

ROCK MELONS: replace with honeydew melons.

SILVERBEET: replace with English spinach.

SNAP PEAS: replace with snow peas (mangetout).

SNAPPER: replace with any firm white fish such as haddock, cod or whiting.

GENERAL INDEX

RECIPE INDEX